# WHERE IS GOD?

James C. Nyemah

Forte Publishing

First Published in 2014

Second Publication 2016
Published by:
**FORTE** Publications
#12 Ashmun Street
Snapper Hill
Monrovia, Liberia


**FORTE** Publishing
7202 Tavenner Lane
# 208 Alexandria
VA, 22306


**FORTE** Press
76 Sarasit Road
Ban Pong, 70110
Ratchaburi, Thailand

http://fortepublishing.wix.com/fppp

This book or any portion thereof may not be reproduced or used in any manner whatsoever without the express written permission of the publisher except for the use of brief quotations in a book review.

Printed in the United States of America

Copyright © 2014 JAME C. NYEMAH
All rights reserved.

ISBN: 0994534728
ISBN-13: 978-0994534729

# DEDICATION

I dedicate this book to my wife, Lucy, and my daughter, Precious, for bearing with me throughout the duration of this great undertaking. Even if no one else will read this book, I know my daughter and I will take turns reading it chapter-by chapter, sharing the stories. Thank you for believing in me.

To all the wonderful people at Africa Faith Expressions - Arizona, I thank you for letting me preach and teach the message in this book to you before publishing it. I remember how we would stay an extra thirty minutes to an hour during our Friday Bible Study to dig a little more into the word of God.

To all the great people of God in Liberia, West Africa, especially to the pastors and churches where I ministered during Missions Liberia (ml) programs in Pleebo, Harper, Zwedru and Monrovia, God bless you. Your ministry greatly encouraged me. To all of the fellowships and associations of churches in these areas, you inspired me.

To my friend, Magdalene Ayorkor Matthews, author of "Rise, Redefining the Future of Liberia," the privilege to read your book before publishing it sent me a good message. Thank you.

# Table of Contents

DEDICATION iii
ACKNOWLEDGMENTS i
INTRODUCTION iii
PART 1 vii
EVERYDAY LIFE vii
CHAPTER ONE 1
When Justice is Needed  1
CHAPTER TWO 14
When Longing for Yesterday or 14
Better Tomorrow Confronts Us 14
CHAPTER THREE 23
When Others Shift Blame on Us  23
CHAPTER FOUR  29
When the Sin(s) of Leaders Suffer the People 29

    a)   Eli and His Sons:  29
    b)   Joshua: 31
    c)   Achan: 32

CHAPTER FIVE 34
When our Past Failure have Caught up with Us 34
CHAPTER SIX  46
When No One Wants to Serve  46

**PART 2  54**
FAMILY PEOPLE  54
CHAPTER SEVEN  55
When Infertility and Abortions Abound  55
CHAPTER EIGHT  59
When Sickness Strikes 59

a. Corporate Wickedness in the Health Industry:  60
b. Corporate Responsibility in Health Industry:  60
  c. Justice and Health Industry:  61
   d. Sickness brings Pain and Anger: 62
    e. Abandonment and Neglect in Sickness:  63

    f.    Illness: Lack of Good Doctors and Hospitals  64
        g.    Being Bewitched by Sickness    64
            h.    Mental Impact of Illness:   66
            i.    There is Hope in Sickness:  66
                CHAPTER NINE    68
                When Death Comes   68
                    a.    Fear of Death    68
                    b.    Dealing with Death    69

**PART 3 73**
PERSONAL 73
CHAPTER TEN 74
When Loneliness Comes    74
CHAPTER ELEVEN 78
When Hope is Lost    78

**PART 4 82**
STORIES THAT QUESTION GOD    82
CHAPTER TWELVE 83
A Sister in Kenya 83
CHAPTER THIRTEEN    86
Cry of a Women Ministry Leader    86
CHAPTER FOURTEEN 89
Ma Phebe and Junior   89
CHAPTER FIFTEEN 94
A Bishop from Kenya  94

**PART 5 98**
UNGRATEFUL HUMANITY 98
CHAPTER SIXTEEN    99
Heaven Asks Ungrateful Humanity  99

**PART 6 103**
CONCLUSION: 103
GOD IS THERE 103
17 CHAPTER SEVENTEEN   105
It Could Be God  105
CHAPTER EIGHTEEN   110
Personal Failures  110

CHAPTER NINTEEN    122
    The Devil    122
CHAPTER TWENTY  134
    You are Not Alone    134

CHAPTER TWENTY-ONE    138
    Press Forward          138
    Bibliography 143
    Born To Take Charge 146
    About the Author 147
ABOUT THE AUTHOR    149

# ACKNOWLEDGMENTS

I can never forget my mother, Rachel Brown, who brought me into this world. Though she was a high school student, she did not agree to kill me through abortion. Though Rachel is my biological mother, I have another mother who nurtured and raised me into the man I am today.

Ma Phebe of Gbiso is my mother, though she is really my grandmother, she is the mother I know. I thank God for my biological father; but he was not really in my life. Pastor Peter K. Nyemah, Ma Phebe's husband, became my real father. I bless God for them. As a child, they gave me love and family.

I had a wonderful childhood. I never lacked anything. Ma Phebe taught me many things about God and life. Besides giving me the privilege to experience miracles daily at Gbiso, she taught me faith, prayer and dedication to God.

Ma Phebe said that life begins with faith; prayer keeps faith, and dedication gives life meaning. Her inspiration helped me greatly over the years. I came to understand that I must know God for myself and not depend on others. I must have faith in God, not in anything else. I have to live a life of dedication to God, if I want God to fulfill his purpose in my life.

Pastor Nyemah taught me about being a man. He said education and hard work makes a man, but women destroy men. To be a man I must get an education because I become what I know. When I know something, I must work at it so I can live by it. And if I am not careful, as good and wonderful women are, they can destroy me easily. It is better to find a woman, marry her and settle down. These words from my wonderful parents have kept me on the path over the years. In my youth, I wandered away from these principles in life and I learned my lesson the hard way. Thanks to God, I remembered my roots and came to my senses, and today I can tell to you.

I thank God for Dr. Maxie Burch, who God used to help me start the church. I appreciate Dr. Dick Stafford at North Phoenix Baptist for believing in me. And, I must say special thanks to Pastor Larrie Fraley at Christ Church of the Valley, who helped bring Missions Liberia to life. After years of prayers and bearing with me, God is still doing his work through me. Thanks for all your prayers and support."

# INTRODUCTION

To ask the question of God's whereabouts seems to suggest finding the geographical location of God. Asking where can easily make one think about the [1] SETI (Search for Extra-Terrestrial Intelligence).

Whether they are trying to find aliens in space or any unknown life in history, the quest of finding life in space exploration could cause one to wonder whether someday humans might find God in space or, somewhere else. To others, this seems to be just good science and not about the futility in thinking about the possibility of finding God through space exploration.

It is not a matter of guessing whether scientists' quest in space, deep waters, or underground, might someday alleviate our burden of finding Heaven or God's dwelling place, so as to find him; but rather, it is a matter of God being there with us in times of need. The heart-wrenching question of finding God has basically little or nothing to do with God's physical address. It is about knowing where God is when life happens to us, and realizing he is there for us.

The question anticipates the presence of God in the midst of our situations. It calls for God coming to us when the alarm sounds, or at least enables us to get in direct contact with him in times of great need, without delay. Life demands great answers to radical questions. We all seek answers literally from every source possible.

All religious people, atheists, Christians and non-believers alike desperately seek answers to life's ultimate questions. Some people try to escape response to this question, by either ignoring it or putting on other forms of pretense. In the meantime, others turn to self-indulgences such as drugs, alcohol and sex. Some other people work too much and become workaholics while some just try to keep a good family together – that's all that matters, they assure themselves. But whatever attempt we might use to answer this question, unfortunately, the need is constant. It does not go away.

Sometimes the needy wonder in despair whether the rich and mighty ever have their share of troubles like they do almost every day. The answer is an astonishing YES! Everyone, including the great and powerful, experience troubles in life; but at different levels and for different reasons.

Sometimes if one looks at the crisis of the rich and mighty, the poor and needy might forget their own plight and say in a great surprise, "wow, we thought those people do not suffer!"

Surely, the poor and needy could express some sympathy for their counterparts. On the other hand, they might laugh at their miseries grudgingly. This makes me remember a Liberian saying that goes, [2] "If you're not inside, you don't know."

The problems we face daily vary. Some problems are physical, like the need for finances, so as to cater to one's personal needs; others are emotional.

They usually hurt on the inside, and by the time that is visible, the damage is great. Others might not lack physically, they might have money, but they are emotionally unstable. They do not sleep well at night, because they are overwhelmed with problems – while some of us can sleep like babies and have good dreams.

Other individual issues are neither physical nor emotional they are spiritual. Most of the time the spiritual lack in a person can manifest itself through physical, psychological and emotional needs.

It shows and overrides the latter, causing the person to suffer. The troubles of life do not have any discrimination. Pain and suffering and all sorts of emotional turmoil face the rich and the poor, the weak and the mighty, at different levels. No one is exempted.

But when it comes to the devout Christian striving for holiness and righteousness in this modern world, (or any religious person for that matter), more questions seem to arise because we have faith and hope in God – or for others, in some higher power. There are also many good people who are not Christians or religious people who just live their lives and do well to assist others in need. But not even these good people are exempted from the troubles of life. This, I think, is heartbreaking.

# WHERE IS GOD?

Christians and all religious people wonder in despair why do certain things happen. They ask, "Why do they happen to us? Are Christians not free from certain ills of life because of our association with God? And, do we have the same fate as non-believers when it comes to pain and suffering in life? If so, then why? And if not, why do we experience negative things anyway? And, where is God in all this? Where is God when life is not fair? Who do we talk to for insight? Where do we go?"

These are all valid questions for the soul in search of answers when life comes at us.

Oh, how much we really wonder in great distress about where God is when we really need him! I think this book will help all of us discover where God is and provide some insight as to why certain things happen. It attempts to explain where God is during those times and what we can do so as not to lose hope and give up, or give in, when they come.

Discovering the place of God in life's complexities will help us find purpose, and the answers to difficult questions. Where is God? The answer is astonishingly ambiguous, because we do not feel or see God in all our situations. Yet, at times he is right there on time, especially when we need him the most. It is not a matter of finding God's current address.

It is about God showing up as our greater refuge and strength in times of trouble. As a matter of fact, who cares where a "Good Samaritan" lives when it comes to an emergency? At least not me; I don't tell someone trying to help me to give me their address before I can be helped. When I have an emergency, I need real help, and that's all!

In our times of need, we want someone to be there, someone to save us: and that is when many people cry out to God and wonder where He is.

So as we can see, the prior knowledge of the origin of help in times of need has no bearing upon lifesaving services that might be rendered to us. This means that all we really need is assistance, not the address of the helper before we can accept their support.

Meanwhile, I believe the angels and the entire hosts of Heaven ask in bewilderment the same question we humans ask in times of distress, asking "Where is God?" There is a sharp difference in the time and manner in which we ask, and when the Kingdom of Heaven asks the same question.

Humanity asks when something is wrong, when we need answers. Unlike this, the angels and the entire Kingdom of Heaven ask when we are enjoying prosperity, good health, good human relations and God's favor. They ask not because they are in need, but rather because many times they see an ungrateful humanity who now has prayers answered and wishes come true, and have quickly forgotten the God who is the originator of all good things.

Therefore, I say this to everyone, God is there, right there!

God is right there even if it looks like he is absent, asleep, or has forgotten about us. He is never too busy to remember us or careless about his responsibility toward us as his children. Even though we may not understand everything about God's presence or his love in times of need, we can rest assured that God is in control and that he has something good in store for each one of us.

# PART 1
# EVERYDAY LIFE

In this section I discussed few things. The issue about justice and injustice and how it affects all of us is quite interesting. The longing we have for the 'good old days' can haunt us when life gets difficult. It is bad to have had good things and later loose them in life. I rather suffer now and enjoy tomorrow than enjoy now and suffer later, especially in my old age. For others, they long for a better tomorrow because their lives are full of sorrow and unfulfilled dreams.

It gets me angry when others shift blame on the innocent for something they did. This is totally unfair. I know that I am not perfect, but suffering for something I did not do, can be a serious problem. Sadly, that can be the case of our leaders and family; their mess in yesterday has a way to affect us in curses today.

One thing that is so sad to see is when our past failures have caught up with us. Even after we have changed and committed to better life; things from the past have a way to show up. It really becomes a pain in our lives when yesterday will not stay in yesterday but shows up today to disturb our present life and tomorrow.

We all like people to serve us. Interestingly, there is a greater joy in serving others that we miss most of the time. When we serve others, we tell them that they matter too; it is not that they are better than us. But we serve out of good will and charity for the common good of humanity.

As you read the first part of this book, all these things will guide you in a time of contemplation. It will challenge you to think again about some things. I pray that you will take some actions in the right direction. Thank you.

# CHAPTER ONE

## When Justice is Needed

We all know how frustrating it can be when justice is not served upon those who well deserved it. We all know the anguish in our souls when we exclaim, "it is not fair!" Regardless of what our morals are and by which standards we measure them, sometimes for unexpected reasons, we are not treated right.

When we complain about fairness, the complaint is legitimate. Every human being has an innate sense of right and wrong by which all cultures articulate their individual norms, morals and laws of society. While the truth remains that many cultures differ in the details of their sense of right and wrong, it is interesting to note that they all become concerned when one does the unexpected by breaking the rules of society.

Justice is a very interesting phenomenon. One may ask, "What is justice?" To begin contemplating this, let us look at the definition from Merriam-Webster's dictionary. [4] Justice (n) 1 a: the maintenance or administration of what is just especially by the impartial adjustment of conflicting claims or the assignment of merited rewards or punishments.

**b**: the administration of law; especially the establishment or determination of administration of rights according to the rules of law or equality.

Consequently, the absence of the maintenance or administration of what is just, especially by [5] the impartial adjustment of conflicting claims or the assignment of merited rewards or punishments is injustice. And the absence of the administration of rights according to the rules of law or equality is also injustice.

But it is not just the absence of doing what is just, it is also doing what is wrong or evil in society. All such things provoke strife that when not taking proper and reasonable steps can lead to a chaotic society wherein peace, stability, and tranquility are only dreams and fantasies that cannot be realized. It should not be so.

When injustice prevails, humans demean one another and violence emerges, which leads only to more violence. Perfect examples of injustice are the wars in West African countries such as Liberia, Ivory Coast, Sierra Leone, or in Pakistan, Iraq, and many other nations. Even though not all injustices lead to wars between countries, or civil wars, some are organizational wars and fierce family feuds that never seem to end.

Injustice, as we have seen, does not have much regard for religion. As a matter of fact, many religions cover up injustice and promote it. When religious ideals are forced upon people who want individual rights to believe or not believe in religion, they are usually treated badly and sometimes put to death in the name of the god of that religion. This has been popular among some mainline religions.

In the early centuries, around the 1500s, Roman Catholics would put to death the Lutherans and Baptists for not believing as they did. Muslims would put to death and mistreat anyone who converted to a different religion, especially to Christianity. Hindus are known to do the same as well. All over the world we see people killing one another in the name of God and of their religion, as if they have no consciences or there were no individual rights in existence.

I see this as a very unfortunate thing looking back at troubling religious wars of the past and current religious wars, just because someone changed their beliefs and state of mind, which many times was for the better. Are people becoming insane nowadays and haven't learned anything from history?

Or is it the eschatology of our individual religions that have blinded our eyes, hardened our hearts and dulled our minds to rightful thinking? Whatever the case, people of integrity must rise up and not allow the injustice of religions, power, greed, selfishness, discrimination or any other type of injustice that encourages us to continually destroy others and our world. We need to spread the word.

While the ideology of Universal Justice or Peace stem from the same root, nevertheless, only few elements of justice can actually be applied universally. There are some issues that concern Universal Justice, things like a person's right to exist, personal safety, right to personal property, and family rights. Such ideals are universal.

People in every culture have the need to co-exist with others, they want to have rights to their personal properties and want to make sure their families are secure and enjoy the privilege of citizenship and rights to residency.

I also understand that the details of justice in one culture do not necessarily apply to the other; they vary. For example, the application of justice in North America relating to the rights of women and children, or traffic violations, is not the same as in Ivory Coast or Liberia in West Africa. Many things for which someone will be apprehended in the USA may not be considered crimes there.

Justice is sometimes coaxed by certain individuals in society. Often it is the rich and powerful who obstruct justice by their status, wealth and power. But on a smaller scale, average citizens seek the easy way out of trouble with the law by bribing the officers who implement the law of society.

Even though we all know that incriminating an innocent person for the sake of releasing the real offender who has relations with people of affluence that can manipulate justice is heartbreaking. However, sadly it is commonplace. In advanced countries law enforcement officers can sometimes plant fabricated evidence to falsely accuse the innocent. What is the excuse that is given for doing this?

Actually, it is a matter of not taking responsibility for one's actions. When someone does wrong, the first thing that comes to mind is the consequences. So when the person and their friends and family understand the penalty for the actions committed, they do not want their friend or relatives to pay for those actions.

As a result, some have resorted to bribe the security officers, lawyers and judges to release the guilty, and/or implicate the innocent. So now, instead of just one crime being committed, family and friends join by obstructing justice through bribes or incriminating the innocent. As the result of this, more crimes are committed than the initial crime, as family and friends set the stage for cover-up.

As the innocent is apprehended, dragged to court, and taken to prison, sometimes being incarcerated for a long time, the criminals go free and the crooked lawyers and judges smile at each other as they enjoy their fat bank accounts as a result of bribes, while the family of the innocent cries for justice and God's intervention. This system is totally ridiculous!

This is where one can ask once more, where is God when the innocent suffers for the guilty and the offender goes free, with the potential of committing more crimes? This is a very sad state of affairs. Why would any rational person let the guilty go free and accuse the innocent? In the justice systems, it is better to close a case than for it to be a mystery. As a matter of fact, the perpetrators are paid to assure peace and security.

In order to fool society, it is easier for them to falsely accuse someone rather than let the case go to the mystery fi les. Or, they would push it under the carpet and do nothing about it, as good citizens cry out for justice. In so doing, a scapegoat is needed. This is where accusing the innocent comes in handy for such people. What a tragedy! Some issues are not a matter of justice; they are not things for people of one culture to freak out over. The issue of marriage is one. While in one culture a woman can marry at age 15, other cultures like North America see it is an abomination.

Actually, when a sexual affair with a 15-year-old is reported to the authorities, the adult becomes guilty of child molestation. This is a serious crime that tarnishes the reputation of the offender for life. Meanwhile, in many African and South American countries, females are engaged to marry or have married by age 15, and it is perfectly normal. The men are so proud of their "sweet 16s" and have big marriage ceremonies. So as you can see, having an affair and taking the hands of 15-year-old females in marriage is not a universal crime.

Therefore, we cannot take our cultural moral measuring tape to try to apply it to other cultures. It just won't work. The pain we may cause might be greater than what we calculate to be the offense. In this regard, we cannot truly say it is not just or right for a man to marry a 15-year-old girl in places where it is totally acceptable and admired, just because our culture frowns upon it. This is not a matter of justice; it is a matter of cultural diversity.

Meanwhile, for example, there are other things that are more prevalent than the qualifications of potential couples. The issue of crimes against the innocent where justice is not done is really critical. Truly, there are times when people are treated badly and their rights are ignored, as their offenders pretend not to realize that they have rights too. Then those people expect their cruelty to be accepted without any remorse.

This is so evil. Sometimes the irony of the innocent suffering while the bad guys go free is quite terrible. Many of us have seen this in a court of law or among common people in everyday life. There has to be someone with divine indignation to stop this!

A righteous man named Job in the Bible once complained about the plight of people suffering that was not given attention while the evildoers were not confronted at all. Job stated that [6] "the groans of the dying rise from the city, and the souls of the wounded cry out for help. But God charges no one with wrongdoing. There are those who rebel against the light, who do not know its ways or stay in its paths. When daylight is gone, the murderer rises up and kills the poor and needy. In the night, he steals forth like a thief." Job was not alone in this frustration!

It pushes my buttons when there is injustice and no one confronts the wrongdoers. But this issue about injustice is not a strange or new concept. It is an old problem that has plagued humanity for thousands of years. Injustice led to slavery, in which people treated other humans of color like animals or machines to work on their cotton and sugar cane farms. Even though there was emancipation in the early 1800s, the issue of injustice still lurks around. Injustice coupled with greed, pride and power led to the slavery of Jews in Egypt a long time ago. It is responsible for the death of six million Jews by the Adolph Hitler during the Holocaust.

It led to religious wars between Roman Catholics and those they called the Protestants, the Lutherans and later the Baptists. Whether injustice is practiced in Latin America by

Europeans or the USA in the early ages, whether it is the West taking advantage of Africa by trading their resources for cheap goods, or for guns to start and support civil wars, or even when leaders hurt their own people, it is wrong. Injustice is a very bad thing regardless of who practices it – we must all fight to stop it.

People of color are still not treated equally in many developed countries across the world. For example, in spite of the fact that in North America there is legislature against discrimination of any sort; people of color know quite well that it still exists in the workplace. Some people of equal qualifications do not get paid equally because of their color or gender.

I worked for a company that started paying me $7.25 an hour and later an Egyptian friend was hired with the same qualifications at $9.00 per hour to start. Of course we were all Africans, he came from Egypt with a light-colored skin similar to Hispanics, while I am a Liberian and Black or Chocolate, whatever people call it. But I guess the light color of my Egyptian friend fooled the employer and they hired him for $1.75 more.

When we discovered this, the two of us just laughed at our employer, thinking it was terribly funny! To us, it was like saying to my friend and I: "James, you make $7.25 because you are black, and you get $9.00 because you are a little bit white! So in short, whites make more money than blacks in some countries, even in the great United States of America.

## WHERE IS GOD?

Some things are an oxymoron and ironic. In the early 1800s, many good-hearted people in North America decided to call on their leaders to ban slavery and thus initiate the emancipation of slaves. As a way to settle this matter, many of the Africans were sent to Liberia in West Africa, a country that got its independence in 1847.

But as these former African slaves from America began to settle in Liberia, some of them had a great idea, to treat their fellow Africans, especially the natives of Liberia, like slaves. Did you hear what I just said? The former slaves who others suffered for to give freedom began to treat others like slaves. These former slaves are known in Liberia as the "Congo people."

Let me explain how this happened. The illiteracy rate in Liberia was very high, especially in those days, and is still high today due to 14 years of civil war. So the natives of Liberia would have their children live with the African-Americans, or Congo people, to educate them. Oh mine, that was not an easy task for the students who lived with the Congo people in Liberia! If you went to live with them, you became their new slave! I don't know whether they were enjoying payback for their years of slavery, but their cruelty lived with the families who had to bear the pain of sending their kids over to them just to be educated.

The husbands and sons of the Congo people sexually molested student servants who lived with them. They were not apprehended for their crimes because it was in Liberia. In addition to that, the police officers, judges and civil authorities were mostly Congo people. Many of them were really wicked to the natives. So, even if you had a case, you were beating a dead horse, because no one would listen to you. They were all the same Uncle Johnny and Aunty Jane. The people of Maryland County, especially in Harper, can testify to this. My aunties, who are still alive, are living witnesses to this cruelty.

This was not just limited to Harper or to Pleebo in Maryland; it was the case in Monrovia as well as other cities across Liberia. If you were living with the Congo people, they made you clean the house, clean the toilets, cook while their own children did nothing, and big mamma watched TV. You see, I made it sound better when I said clean the toilets. When I say toilet, what I mean is not the usual Western toilet we have.

It was something like what we use today to potty-train kids, usually a small item like a bucket or big bowl with a top. When they had bowel movements in the night, the student servants had to wash and thoroughly clean the toilet by daybreak. If you forgot to do that task on time, they would spill the nasty poop on your face! Did you hear me? If you did not clean up after them on time, you got poop dumped right in your face! One of my aunties had to suffer this terrible ordeal just for her education. Oh, what cruelty they endured for education!

This was not all there was to it. After the house was cleaned, they would hardly give the servants food to eat, much less appreciate them. For many Congo people, it was like working for your education as they once had worked on a sugar cane or cotton farm in America. Many times after the servants cooked, they were not allowed to eat with the family. As the Congos reclined at the dinner table, the student servants had to wait on them. And many times they got little or nothing to eat. Every good thing that their student servant did was credited to their own children, who actually did nothing.

It is no wonder that in 1980 the natives overthrew the Congo-led government, which began the civil war that lasted for more than a decade, with quarter of a million people killed.

The infrastructure was destroyed and national resources plundered by various brutal rebel factions. I pray that Liberia will have peace and justice; and fight corruption.

Why did I discuss the case of the Congo people of Liberia treating their fellow countrymen like slaves is oxymoron? Well, these Congo people known in America today as African-Americans had just been released from cruel hard labor, where they thirsted, being molested, raped and murdered by their slave masters in America, only go to Liberia and treat others just like slaves again! Let the world hear this. Such things did happen before and are still happening in Liberia today.

What a tragedy when poor and needy people treat one another bad. Even today our modern societies would not allow anyone to treat animals, much less humans, so inhumanely.

But the African-Americans did that to their fellow Liberians, and these atrocities still go on today. This reminds me of a story in the Bible about the unmerciful servant. Jesus, speaking to his followers about trespasses and forgiveness said, [7]"Therefore, the kingdom of heaven is like a king who wanted to settle accounts with his servants. As he began the settlement, a man who owed him ten thousand talents was brought to him. Since he was not able to pay, the master ordered that he and his wife and his children and all that he had be sold to repay the debt.

The servant fell on his knees before him. 'Be patient with me,' he begged, 'and I will pay back everything.' The servant's master took pity on him, canceled the debt and let him go.

But when that servant went out, he found one of his fellow servants who owed him a hundred denarii. He grabbed him and began to choke him. 'Pay back what you owe me!' he demanded. His fellow servant fell to his knees and begged him, 'be patient with me, and I will pay you back.' But he refused. Instead, he went off and had the man thrown into prison until he could pay the debt. When the other servants saw what had happened, they were greatly distressed and went and told their master everything that had happened."

In this story, a servant owed his master money he could not pay. It was lawful for him and his family to be taken as slaves to cover the debt. As you just read, after he begged for mercy, his master completely forgave him all his debt. What a good master! On the contrary, he found his fellow servant who owed him and could not afford to pay right away. He refused to grant his friend forgiveness or give him time to repay, but unmercifully threw him in prison. What a cruel guy!

I added this to say that the Congo people of Liberia were once former slaves in America. People of good heart freed them and sent them back to Liberia where they could have freedom and liberty. But just like the cruel servant whose master forgave his debt, the African-Americans (called the Congo people in Liberia) began to find new slaves for themselves by using their student servants as slaves!

That is terrible! After many clergies, civil leaders and good people fought hard for their freedom, they enslaved others. This was very tyrannical. It is a common fact that it is not just the rich and powerful practice injustice; ordinary people do also. I believe that all of those who fought for the emancipation of African slaves would feel quite terrible about what the African-Americans did to the Liberian people. Injustice is evil and it should be the moral obligation of every person to ensure justice, peace and stability for the betterment of us all, not allow such evil to take place in society.

Wouldn't it be nice if our world treated people equally in the workplace and social atmosphere based on their knowledge, gifts and abilities, instead of being discriminated against because of their color or gender? Our world would be so much better! It is sad to know that the opposite is commonplace. Discrimination is alive and well, whether it is racial, gender or class; and it is real. If you do not believe this, then take a poll and ask some people of color or gender about their experiences and view on this. It would give you some insight into these terrible crimes.

When I think about injustice, I think in broad terms. It makes no difference upon which scale this is practiced; it is still a wicked thing. Whether it is a parent favoring one child over the others, or husbands cheating on their wives while expecting them to be faithful, injustice cannot be warranted. It is still evil. In today's fast-paced world, education is very important, but the problem comes when some students are not promoted through the standards set forth by the school systems in various countries.

Instead of students studying and passing their tests in order to be promoted and graduate from their course of study, teachers, students and parents seem to have another grand idea. It is called the "short-cut," I call it "short-cut" because it is not the proper way to help students become successful, but it is apparently the quick and easy way out. Teachers and students sometimes engage in sexual affairs to get a good grade. Wow, sex for grades? This is totally ridiculous!

This behavior is prohibited in the school systems, yet it happens. It is not fair when other students have taken the time to do their research and study, while others engage in sex to get a good grade. This is one of the tragedies of wicked countries. This tragedy takes place both in third-world countries and in well-developed countries. Nevertheless, school systems do well to promote the Fairness Act and disciplines those caught doing these things– if they can catch them.

The other problem about injustice in schools is bribery. Students and parents bribe teachers to get passing grades.

When this happens, the result is evident in the workplace. Such corrupt systems produce employees who do not know the job well because they did not actually pass the requirements to obtain their licenses and lied about their qualifications. Working with such people can be a pain in the body. Injustice exists in sports and entertainment as well. In sports, it can result in riots and huge controversies when, for instance, a foul is not counted by the referee. In advanced places, the referee can get in serious trouble over such things, but in other places, the problems this causes can be overwhelming.

Sometimes when the wrong person or people are awarded first place in a competition, the commotion can be so substantial. There is no need for cheating in these cases. I see that injustice is practiced more often in poor countries. The national resources are sometimes limited, yet they are still misappropriated by government agencies. Think about this, when the government that should be "for the people and by the people" cheats the people, how bad can this get! It all makes me sick to my stomach. Because power is on their side, the poor are silenced as the so-called strong and mighty use government money intended for developmental projects to party or womanize, or other selfish ambitions!

I saw this in Liberia and other places. No wonder the result of this and other issues was a terrible senseless 14-year civil war which destroyed about a quarter of a million people, the national infrastructure, and displaced many, forcing them into refugee camps in neighboring countries, including Ghana, Ivory Coast and some in Sierra Leone and Guinea. One may ask the leaders of poor third-world countries the question, why do you misuse funds intended to help your country for selfish gain? They would actually not be able to answer; they would feel guilty, speechless and give some senseless unprepared excuse.

It is not fair that people do not receive the same and equal punishment for the same crimes committed. The rich and powerful are treated differently from the poor and needy, or even middle class, in the courts of law in many countries. Both the rich and powerful bribe the authorities and go free or receive less punishment than the poor without the money to bribe. Shouldn't justice be blind to discrimination in relation to status, gender, religion or ethnicity? Oh how I wish this was really so, but unfortunately the opposite is true in many cases! Oh God, where are you?

Again, the issue of injustice is a grave problem, whether it is practiced on a large or small scale, it does not matter. It does not matter who engages in it, it can bring confusion, and at the most, wars can happen because of this. Many civil wars in Africa and other places derived from injustice. When the rich and powerful are mistreating the poor and suffering, it is not fair, or whether it is the poor and needy strangling each other, it is still not fair. We must fight to stop such indecencies.

Human beings have the right to exist freely and do what they want in the confines of good governing. I did not say "in the confines of the law" because slavery in North America was lawful, even though evil and immoral – it was dehumanizing. Good governance comes into play when the individual rights of the people are well proportioned by authority, and each person has their civil liberties. This reminds me of the National Anthem of Liberia which states [8] "in union strong success is sure – we cannot fail!"

This implies that when we are united, justice is served equally to everyone without discrimination and success is sure, meaning we cannot fail. But when injustice prevails, strife arises and trouble begins to brew into the terrible and revolting soup of war. Let us all do our part to be fair to one another in public arenas, in families, or in groups of any size.

Justice is one thing we all need in spite of our culture, ethnicity, religion or gender. We all deserve to be treated right.

Don't we all deserve justice? Yeah, we all need justice. The cost of damage caused by injustice far surpasses the cost of just treatment of others. We do not have to suffer humanity in this manner. I challenge all of us to follow what Christians call the Golden Rule, a command from Jesus Christ which says [9] "so in everything, do to others what you would have them do to you, for this sums up the Law and the Prophets." It sums up the law because if we treat one another with equal respect and dignity in the same manner we would like to be treated; our countries would not have to spend billions of dollars for national security. These funds could be used for education and other developments, or even medical research.

It sums up the prophets because religious people, in spite of their respective nationalities, and their faith in God should increase their awareness of the moral decisions they make in a world that is sometimes corrupt and depraved. Religious people cannot hide behind their religions and commit crimes against humanity in the name of their god or religion.

A crime is a crime, whether it is committed in the church or in a stripper bar! It does not matter whether a pastor committed it or a ruthless gang did. The people who commit crimes and the places they are committed makes it no less a crime. Therefore, the social, moral and religious aspect of self-respect and dignity for humanity should be preserved properly, with fairness for all. This is vital for our peaceful co-existence with one another in society. Justice does not only give us peace, it allows us to enjoy diversity and tranquility. In our world today I know we understand what the absence of justice means. Let us all work together and fight injustice on behalf of humanity. Let us do this for ourselves and for the future of our children. We deserve a better world. They deserve a better world. Let justice reign.

# CHAPTER TWO

## When Longing for Yesterday or Better Tomorrow Confronts Us

There are times in life when we all want to take a break from our miseries and enjoy life just a little bit without the daily headaches we face. We all want to make some improvements in our lives. Whether it is simple things or great moves, we want to move from point A to point B for a better tomorrow. Some who take the metro bus would love to own a vehicle and not have to endure hot summers and cold winters at the bus stops or train stations.

Others want to settle down in a loving and respectful relationship and stop the dating game where they have not found true love. They want to get that promotion from one night-stands and dinner dates. They want to find someone they can spend time with whenever they want, so they can please each other at their convenience.

The poor want to improve their finances to help their families. People prefer not to live from paycheck-to-paycheck; it is obviously better to be able to save some money for the future.

They want to send their kids to better schools and enjoy family and holiday dinners, or make some needed home and self-improvements. Middle class families want to climb the ladder of life and not be stuck living in neighborhoods that are turning violent with gunfire shots almost every night. They would love to be able to move into a nice, quiet place where each household respects themselves and others.

We all know the feeling to want something we do not have because of lack of resources. Oh, how much our hearts can burn without any quench to satisfy our longings, and it is quite miserable. It might be that we had it before and lost it, or we want something new and better. If either is true, our frustration level can be high. Losing a loved one, our job, an important asset, or missing out on a great opportunity can be a major heartbreak.

A man in the Bible named Job had such longing and endless frustration in his soul when he said in anguish, [10] "Oh, for the days when I was in my prime, when God's intimate friendship blessed my house. When I went to the gate of the city and took my seat in the public square, whoever heard me spoke well of me, and those who saw me commended me, because I rescued the poor who cried for help, and the fatherless who had none to assist him."

Job was a good man who lost it all. He lost his children, his valuable property, and then his health, but the worst of all for Job was when his wife turned her back on him and asked him to do the unthinkable so he could die and not suffer any more. It was quite terrible for Job. What made it really depressing was the sequence of the events, yet Job kept his faith and remained steadfast without giving up.

There are times when we really miss intimate relationships we had with friends, families and loved ones. Our desire to rekindle those broken or gone-forever relationships leaves scars upon our souls. We miss these people when an issue has destroyed our friendship or broken up our home. We miss them when the clutches of death have stolen them from us for eternity.

When it really hurts, sometimes people never get back on their feet again due to the impact of the loss. For Job, he missed the good relationship he had with God as his friend. He found himself in a place where it seemed that God had forgotten all about him or did not care about his affairs. How many of us today feel the heavy burden of neglect and rejection? I know it truly hurts. Throughout this turbulent time, Job's heart would always revert to the good old days when life was at its pinnacle. He reminisced about the days he was in his prime. He had good friends, and of course, those who were just there to take advantage of him. He was well respected among his peers. Job was also benevolent. He helped the poor and blessed them with things they needed. Job was not only rich and powerful, but he was a good citizen.

In spite of all Job was, his share of misery finally arrived. It was then that Job began to remember the times when life was better. When his soul could not find rest as he sought for a better tomorrow to end his terrible life, he grieved for the good old days.

King Solomon, who was considered the king of wisdom in Israel in ancient times wrote, [11] "I know that there is nothing better for men than to be happy and do good while they live." Of course, many scholars and philosophers debate about what is the highest good. From Socrates to Aristotle to Kant, all of them seem to agree that the greatest good for a man is not a means to an end; it is an end in itself. It is not enough to gain another thing. But it is good in that its possession moves one to a place of peace and tranquility without more desire to want. For example, one may work for a good education to obtain a better job, make more money and live a better life.

So here, the education is a means to the better job, and the better job is a means to a better life. But even the better life in itself is not the final destiny. The greatest good would then be the achievement of something that erases our desire to want. It is actually what we wanted, not what we receive or do to get what we want. Suffice it to say that the greatest accomplishment of mankind is happiness.

This happiness is not just dependent upon something taking place that would make us happy. It is not happiness when we tell someone if you do what I want, then I will be happy. In this definition of happiness, it is the end itself with no departures.

Even though true happiness can be achieved by a succession of events, it is not solely dependent upon such happenings.

It was this sort of happiness King Solomon talked about when he said that nothing is better under the sun than for men to be happy. But when a heavy cloud of darkness or trouble overshadows us, finding happiness in this light can be very difficult.

Notwithstanding, there are some people who know how to stay happy regardless of what life brings them. But I tell you, the currents of destruction that they have to withstand can be immense.

So King Solomon was saying that being happy is good for mankind. Meanwhile, we all know that all the billions of people in the world today are not even close to happy. What a misery! But many of us who experiences difficult times that blur our vision to true happiness, know the longing in our souls to become happy and experience life in its fullness. Who doesn't want to get a break from hard times? Come on, we all do!

We all want a better life than what we have possibly lived before, or what we are living now, or just to recreate the good old days again and relive our dreams. But when such dreams cannot be realized, our heart breaks and all we can do is either sit back and accept things the way they are, or just keep fighting until the changes occur.

For most of us, this longing for a better tomorrow lost in yesterday, or reaching the place of meaning, purpose, and fulfillment can be a lifelong quest. Regardless, we can still keep the faith and not give up in life just because things are not what we want right now. I would rather say, in the midst of our conflicts and unfulfilled dreams and visions, let the struggle to a better tomorrow continue. Let us press on until we can achieve our dreams.

Let's be frank, not all good relationships that were lost in the past can be rekindled. This may either be because everything has changed, or the other person has moved on with their life and excluded us. Or maybe the clutches of death have taken them away forever. Whether the group you associated with does not exist anymore or that broken relationship turned into a lost opportunity that will never be realized, please do yourself a favor, and move on!

Could it be that you had great romantic intimacy with someone special, or a business relationship that no longer exists? It might be some greater heights you enjoyed in your life that only seem to be a dream now, or even a special closeness you had with God, whatever that missing bond, special person or group was, you can do yourself a favor by accepting the fact that things have changed and you must make all necessary adjustments to move on.

Don't live in yesterday; life is too short to languish, so move on. If you lost a loved one, I am sorry. Was it a friend, family member or spouse, or a special someone? Even if it was the opportunity of your life in your career, please accept my sympathy and do not beat yourself up so badly for that which is already gone. Sometimes life is just that way. Bad things happen to good people, and they happen to everyone.

Many times, poor or middle class people do face life's difficulties more than their rich and powerful counterparts do; when trouble strikes they do not have anyone to bail them out.

Lack of resources can limit them in so many painful ways and that can be heartbreaking. While the impact of the sorrows of life varies from one person or group to the other, one fact remains, that bad things happen to everyone, and whether we admit or not, the impact is there.

One question that remains in this case is the whereabouts of God when all we can do is regret the past we miss so badly, or keep longing for a better tomorrow that seems to be out of reach. Oh, Heaven hear us, things like this are quite frustrating, and give many of us sleepless nights and long days as we try our hardest to make things better.

Notwithstanding, I believe that one day our tears will be wiped away. I also believe that our dreams for a better tomorrow will become a full reality by the help of God. You can make it, so do not give up too soon. Please understand that regardless of how difficult this might be for you, my dear friend, do not abandon your dreams. I know there is someone who watches over you and sees your hardship. He understands your struggles, and has a plan for you.

He will strengthen your heart or someone will appear very soon to bring you peace and tranquility. He will answer your prayers. Just know that the situation will change, and things will get better. The sleepless nights and unquenchable tears you have been dealing with will turn into a time of testimony, story-telling and laughter. So what am I telling you? God will be there to help you through, so please do not give up.

Let me tell you something. Just like you who have issues, I have my share of troubles, missed opportunities, a shameful past, and a time when I was a bit wild. I was ignorant and arrogant – what a terrible combination that leads to sheer foolishness and self-destruction. I was a terrible mess. I allowed my youthful passions to drive me crazy. I let others control my life instead of living a life of purpose and meaning. But things are not that way anymore, so I will give you just a glimpse of my story. The Lord delivered me from my life of self-destruction, regrets and failure, to a life of meaning. And he can do the same for you today!

While I have not yet attained the fullness of life –I am far from it – I can describe for you what I have become versus the past, and compare that to what most of my peers are doing today. I can clearly say without pride and apologies that I am way ahead of the game in many areas than some of my friends.

God is a respecter of no one and what he has done for me he can do for you as well. Hold onto God. Between you and me, many other people in our lifetime have truly not had the great opportunities we had.

It is not the longing for the good old days, but a yearning for a better tomorrow. As life brings us the good and the bad through people, places and situations, the big difference is "us." We can be the difference. The main thing is our reactions and response to life as it happens. Do we accept the facts and then work hard to make our own history, or do we allow history to take us along in its relenting continuum as we sit back blaming others without charting the course for our lives?

Ask yourself these questions: "how did I respond when this happened? Did I properly handle it with all of the available resources, or did I get stuck in it? Or maybe did I simply fall to the ground crying like a little baby?" While these questions might seem irrelevant to many of us, this could be the very reason we have remorse about our past, as we continue our struggle today.

So where is God when our soul longs impatiently for a better life? Let's find out together. Could it be that God is teaching us a lesson about patience or trying to make us humble? Consider this; some are too proud because they don't have much, like the people in high places we know. It could be that God is teaching us a valuable lesson we did not realize before, about something wonderful called "humility." This could be an attribute we need to change in our lives, something that has held us down or made us less productive in our public or religious service.

Pride can even undermine our businesses and relationships. This is something we need to be cognizant of. I understand the presence of evil in this world, and the misery we suffer many times for so long, undeservingly, but I have seen God utilize bad experiences in our lives as testimony to help others in similar conditions, or even worse.

The difference is sometimes as simple as changing our attitude, especially about things over which we have little or no control. I wonder if you are not one of the people who let your attitude cloud your judgment and made rash decisions which complicated things even more. Are you among the group who keep malice and grudges for others because of misunderstandings?

Please stop blaming others for your troubles; forgive and move on – you will do yourself a great favor by letting go of the past and moving on to something new that will benefit you.

Do you realize that every time you see the person or people you feel let you down and who you are not willing to forgive, you get in a bad mood?

I want you to understand that this can hurt you and cloud your judgment toward anyone with whom you have unresolved issues. Please let it go and move on with your life. Make it is about you and not them. It is so easy to blame others for the unfortunate things that happened to us, but we should check ourselves to see whether we possibly contributed to it as well. It is easy to see the faults of others, rather than our own wrongdoing that put us where we are today.

Good things happen to both good and wicked people, to the rich and mighty, as well as the poor and suffering. What counts most is our response, especially when we accept the facts and work hard to change the course of our lives toward our own betterment.

So what about all of this longing for change? This is what I choose to say to all of us caught up in this fateful situation, "Please carefully consider what you gain from this material and many other great resources that are available. I am sorry that bad things happened to you and you have regrets about yesterday, and are longing for a better tomorrow. I wish I had a quick-fix, but life is not so." Most of us are not born rich, and even the rich have their share of troubles. Living in deprivation all the time can be a great tragedy. Here is something to consider: life happens, good and bad.

Let us adjust accordingly and move on. People or things we have lost may not come back to us, and even if they did come, situations might not be the same now. Please understand and make things a little easier for yourself. Times are changing fast and we must all adjust. We all get old and things do not remain the same forever. Sometimes change is necessary. Instead of crying for yesterday, why don't we work today for a better tomorrow? I think that will better help us to succeed than mourning the past; let us learn to see the big picture.

In relationships, an old lover might have treated you in a certain way that your new spouse or special someone is not doing. Please accept my apology, forget the past and do what you have to, to make things work. Do not live in yesterday with regret and complaining. Do something creative and meaningful today to see how you can make the situation enjoyable and fulfilling. Both of you can learn what pleases the other and adapt new methods to make things even better than what you remember from before. It is all up to you.

This same methodology and creativity about romantic relationships is transferrable to family, business and different groups, including church or clubs. If yesterday is gone, let's learn from our mistakes and move on. Living in regret daily will soon affect your social relations, work, family and even your health.

It does not do us any good other than bringing anger and frustration, which could lead to depression, suicide or other negatives outcomes. I want for you to cheer up. Please do something more meaningful in your life now and move on.

There are some of us who not only need to accept that facts, cry over them if necessary, move on and forget them, but we must fight for what is rightfully ours. If you are able to fight for a change, I encourage you to fight with all your might and explore every possible resource to achieve your goal.

If this is you, my dear, I will be praying for your restoration and new development. I will join you in prayers so that God can help you through it. It may not be easy, but I believe it is something you can do when you are determined. Some of us need to stay strong in the face of adversity to get back our families, jobs, ministry and other important things.

This battle for restoration, hope and destiny is not a small one. It calls for tough resolutions, persistence and prayers. While we can solicit help from our churches, families and friends, the victory sometimes calls for personal sacrifice. We must fight very hard for the people and things that are precious to us. I must be frank with you, though, sometimes this is the fight of our lives, but *we've gotta' do what we've gotta' do!* I will be praying for you, and know you are not alone.

# CHAPTER THREE

## When Others Shift Blame on Us

Today we live in a world wherein not many of us really want to take responsibility for our actions. It is easier to blame others or just give meaningless excuses for something we have done. I believe we all know the frustration and anger we experience when someone have done something wrong and they are not accepting the result of their actions, especially when it is something that affects us.

However, before you and I can bash others about what they may have done, let us do a reality check about ourselves and see how well we compare to others. Let me ask you few questions to refresh your mind. Have you ever lied on your little brother or sister, or even a friend about something you did?

Have you lied before to get out of trouble, even if it was just a small lie? Have you ever blamed other people about things that happened to you to which you contributed? Have you lied to a police officer or other authorities to save yourself? Do you think other people are responsible for how life is treating you now without your own personal contribution? If you answered yes to any or all of the questions above, I think you have some idea about why many people lie or blame others for things they do. If you answered no to all of the above, I hope you are not lying. This is not a test for a grade in school to cheat on. I just want to test your honesty.

It is possible that there are some people who could truly and honestly answer no to all of the above questions and be honest about it, but for many of us, I think we understand how our little blaming game can turn into a bigger and more dangerous scheme for others. Whether it is children doing something and blaming it on their siblings or parents blaming actions on their kids, or sex offenders blaming their victims, whatever the case may be, shifting blame on others for what we did is a dishonest thing. It is discouraging to see how people blatantly lie and blame others for their actions. Many people do not want to take responsibility for their own actions. Sadly, many of us have done this before or we are still doing it even as we read this material.

I have discovered that this is nothing new. It didn't just start in our modern world with the advance of technology that makes cover-ups easier. The shifting of blames or bold denial goes as far back as we can remember. It started long ago in primitive times.

The Bible holds an account of Adam and Eve, the first people in the world according to the Holy Scriptures, where they began our misery of being dishonest when answering questions, shifting blames, and cover-up. This issue has plagued humanity for thousands of years. Moses, the author and leader of people of Israel wrote in the Bible that **[12]** the LORD God formed man from the dust of the ground and breathed the breath of life into his nostrils, and the man became a living being. The LORD God planted a garden in the east, in Eden, and there he put the man he had created. And the LORD God made all kinds of trees and plants to grow out of the ground—trees that were pleasing to the eye and good for food. In the middle of the garden were the tree of life and the tree of the knowledge of good and evil. The LORD God put the man in the Garden of Eden to take care of it. And the LORD God commanded the man, "You are free to eat from any tree in the garden, but you must not eat from the tree of the

Knowledge of good and evil, for when you eat of it you will surely die." The LORD God said, "It is not good for the man to be alone. I will make a helper suitable for him." Then the LORD God made a woman from the rib of the man, and he brought her to the man.

In this account, the man named Adam was created by God and given responsibility to cater to the garden. God saw that he was lonely, so God created Eve as his partner, and Adam and Eve both began to enjoy the garden as a newly wedded couple and enjoyed themselves.

But in a short time, the whole story changed and their romance and honeymoon was cut short by the presence of the cunning serpent.

This is the account: [13] Then the man and his wife heard the sound of the LORD God as he was walking in the garden in the cool of the day, and they hid from the LORD God among the trees of the garden. But the LORD God called to the man, "Where are you?" He answered, "I heard you in the garden, and I was afraid because I was naked; so I hid." And he said, "Who told you that you were naked? Have you eaten from the tree that I commanded you not to eat from?"

The man said, "The woman you put here with me—she gave me some fruit from the tree, and I ate it." Then the LORD God said to the woman, "What is this you have done?" The woman said, "The serpent deceived me, and I ate."

Reread the scriptures when God asked Adam where he was. Adam did not just answer by saying, "Lord, I am hiding behind the tree or bushes," but rather he became loquacious. Instead of just saying where he was, guilt made him to talk too much by saying that he heard God in the garden, he was afraid, and so he hid. Stop there; this is too much information. Maybe Adam thought his many words could have save him, but when he realized his many words brought more questions, he resorted to blaming Eve.

When he stated that he was naked, God asked him how he knew that he was naked and questioned him about the forbidden tree. Right away Adam said to God that the woman God had put there with him was responsible. Don't you like how he pretends not to even know the woman when he said to God that the woman you put here gave me the fruit and I had no choice but to eat it? Adam appeared to be a smart guy, but was he that smart? Not only did he refused responsibility for his actions, he implicated God first by saying to God that it was the fault of the woman you put here.

This simply means that when he was here all alone there was no trouble until God made the mistake by bringing the woman, now we see the results! He continued to say that the woman God put there gave him the fruit, meaning that he did not just pick the fruit and ate it. Eve was his evil accomplice who should be responsible, not him.

Wow, what a genius guy named Adam who just "released" himself from trouble by implicating God and his wife, Eve! Good job Adam, that's right! I hope you have not forgotten the time when you were in Eden all alone. You did not have a companion, and you were lonely and probably miserable because nothing of your kind existed in all creation at that time.

It is true that there was no trouble, but God saw how miserable and lonely you were and brought you a beautiful wife you named Eve and adored very much. You refused to take charge and let things get out of control by Eve's acceptance from the serpent and proposal to you, yet you now decide to blame God and forget the recent sweet honeymoon you were enjoying without speaking harshly to God. How can you forget so soon and start pointing fingers now? Come on, Adam, let us be real.

When God's first creation, Adam the man, shifted the blame, what do you expect little Eve to do? Accept the responsibility when the man did not do so? Oh no, not Eve! Remember how a little child would tell their mother or father, "when I grow up I want to be just like mommy or daddy." They hardly ever say "I want to be like God." So Eve, wanting to be "good" like Adam, did just what her husband had done by blaming the serpent, which also settled the implication that since God put the serpent in the garden, thus He was responsible.

As a result, the woman told God that the serpent deceived her, meaning that she did not do it on her own. So all God needed to do was to handle the serpent, not them. This is one good way to trace the origin of this phenomenon and not hold anyone responsible for their own actions. It appears that Adam and Eve were very shrewd, although not too smart like they might have thought about themselves. For Adam and Eve, their little blaming game did not work. It was no match for God's judgment, because God punished all three of them – Adam, Eve and the serpent – for their disobedience, lies and denial of responsibility. Oh how I wish the story was a little different since it has affected mankind forever!

How I wish I had lived in the Garden of Eden to experience the magnificence of God's glory and his physical companionship with Adam and Eve. But thanks be to God that there is hope through Jesus Christ, the Second Adam, who came to restore the broken relationship between mankind and God for eternity. And now humanity can have companionship with God and experience Him as it was before.

Blaming others for our mistakes is a very bad habit. Others may even be killed because of that. Many male sex offenders have often blamed females or their victims for encouraging the man to molest them. They claimed they couldn't help themselves. The victim was so sexy and beautiful, and all they wanted to do was have sex and enjoy themselves, not to hurt the victims, even though it was without their consent.

Child molesters and rapists make such claims as they refuse to be held accountable, and blame the victims for their beauty. What a cruelty! Male sex offenders can force and rape women and children and then tell the authorities that they could not resist their beauty! This is so evil, but unfortunately, it has become commonplace today. Whether the game of blaming others is for violent crimes like rape or molestation, or just blaming your spouse or sibling for simple things, it is still unscrupulous. Whether it is done on local, national or international levels, it is still deadly. It hurts others. We all need to fight to stop this!

Using innocent people as scapegoats for our evil plans

demeans people. It has the potential to make us feel superior over others. Paying poor people to blame themselves in our legal systems for things we did is despicable. This dirty deed hurts others and our communities.

The way to a better world begins with responsibility and accountability. It begins with a world of good morals as we respect ourselves and others equally. Please let all of us work tirelessly to stop shifting blame for the things we do. The blame game is quite terrible. Another person should not have to suffer the penalty for our wrongdoing. We need to be fair.

# CHAPTER FOUR

# When the Sin(s) of Leaders Suffer the People

### a) Eli and His Sons:

The story of Eli, a priest who served God in Israel for many years, is a clear example of good public leadership which failed at home. Eli was a very powerful man of God. He raised the Prophet Samuel who exterminated the practice of witchcraft and divination throughout Israel and anointed Saul and David as king over Israel.

As powerful a leader and priest Eli was, he failed to train his children. Despite the complaints the elders and people of Israel brought before him concerning the bad behavior of his sons, Eli did not do much to rebuke or discipline them. The weakness and sins of the priest, Eli, brought a lot of trouble upon Israel. 1430,000 men died in battle; the Ark of the Covenant, which represented the very presence of God in their midst, was captured by their enemies, the Philistines; his two sons died in battle, his daughter-in-law gave birth by force; and in the end, upon hearing about the capture of the Ark, Eli broke his neck and died!

I must ask this question. Was it worth it, Eli? I guess he forgot or overlooked the proverb that says, "When you spare the rod, you spoil the child." The Bibles says that [15] "Whoever spares the rod hates their children, but the one who loves their children is careful to discipline them."

For Israel, it was not just about spoiling the children; it was mass murder of 30,000 men leaving behind widows and orphans, the death of two princes, though corruption, the death of their leader, and worst of all, the capture of the Ark, which had represented the presence of God among them!

What a loss, Eli! For not taking care of business at home, Eli's carelessness in properly training two boys rained much havoc on the nation. It became a national tragedy. I am left to wonder how Israel felt about the calamity the house of their leader, Eli, brought upon them. Did it go something like this during his funeral? "Oh Eli, we love you, but you and your sons destroyed our nation and our pride, and even the Ark of the Covenant is taken, thanks to you."

Or were they somehow empathetic towards him by saying: "he was a good man, but he allowed his hard-headed children to destroy him and our country. We will never want to have another leader like you!" Or perhaps Israel was crying and saying, "oh God, where are you?"

Meanwhile, let us examine a few things that went wrong. The emphasis of Eli's ministry, work and profession was toward outsiders, yet he neglected his own family. His work apparently impacted his home in a negative way. Perhaps the expectation of Eli was that his sons would "get it" by being around him, and seeing his good work and leadership, without actually teaching them how to live decent and orderly lives as princes.

The other thing we can say about Eli is that he did not practiced in his home what he preached at church. It seemed like he compartmentalized his work and family life. I want to believe Eli was so caught up in his work and ministry so much so that he did not give proper attention to his own family. He blinded himself to his failure by being busy doing the Lord's work, only to see in the end that his family destroyed him.

Earlier I said I would have asked Eli a few questions about his profession and family life, and about the terror that came upon Israel because of his negligence of being a good father to the detriment of the nation. But let me ask few questions before you and I batter the priest Eli for his mistakes. How many times have we neglected our home and families in the name of work or ministry? How many of the children's events, including choir performances, sports games, spelling bees, play or lunch dates have we missed? Or to those of us in relationships, how many times were we not there when our partner needed us which led to some unnecessary quarrels. Perhaps, there were extra attachments outside our relationships? How many times have we failed those we love by our silence, absence or harshness?

I think by looking at our own lives, we see how we have failed many people, including our family and other loved ones. I believe all of those people are wondering somewhere in the corner, and asking: "God where are you when this person is neglecting me? Does it have to be so? No! The application of a little rebuke and discipline would have rescued the children from their wayward lives and saved Eli and his household, along with the nation Israel, a lot of despair. I hope we all can learn something from this story before we make this disgusting statement in regret one day, "Had I known . . ."

There are many other people and stories to discuss regarding the failure of leaders and the devastation it can cause to a family, friends and in fact, a nation. As I bring you few more characters, I want all of us to keep in mind our own mistakes that sometimes cost us so much. I know it is easy to talk about what others have done and forget what we might have done if some of us were in those situations, perhaps we would have done worse.

### b) Joshua:

Joshua was a brave young leader who succeeded the great leader of Israel, Moses. Moses parted the Red Sea, Joshua parted the river Jordan when it was overflowing and let the children of Israel into the promised land of Canaan. Joshua's mandate was to conquer the land and make it the dwelling place of Israel, as the God of their forefathers had promised them. But somewhere during his conquest, before he knew it, Joshua made a deal with the people of Gibeon he was to fight the next day. [16] Joshua made a treaty of peace with them to let them live, and the leaders of the assembly ratified it by oath.

The enemies dressed in rags and came with rotten food and stated that they came from afar, and wanted peace with Israel so that their land wouldn't be destroyed. Without asking God about this great decision, young Joshua accepted the deal and made a peace covenant with the Gibeonites. Sadly, the next day Joshua realized these deceitful people came from the town where he was going to battle.

Joshua tried to break the covenant, but God warned him that it would mean death to Israel. As terrible as Joshua felt about this lie and betrayal, he was forced to accept these people while knowing that their religion, customs and social life would negatively impact Israel. In his last speech to Israel, Joshua hinted at the possibility of idolatry and disobedience to God that partially came from his mistake. I believe this was a regret Joshua lived with until he died.

### c) **Achan:**

If the last two stories did not get your attention, let me give you a summary of few more. The story of Achan is heart-wrenching. Achan was one of the men who fought with Joshua during the conquest of Canaan. God had ordered them to destroy everything and take no captives or spoils. But somewhere along the way after their victory, Achan became disobedient and greedy and stole some items. Because of the theft, Israel lost 36 men to a small town called Ai. The living soldiers were badly disgraced and had to run for their lives. The interesting part of the story was that as Israel mourned for the dead, Joshua wept before the Lord and asked why this had to happen. The Lord revealed to Joshua that it was because of Israel's sin, so Joshua should rid the people of the sin.

The next morning, they cast lots and the lots fell to Achan. The penalty for Achan's sin was that Achan, and his sons and daughters, together with the stolen items, as well as his cattle, donkeys, tent and all he had, were stoned to death and burned. Enough for justice! Were all these people supposed to bear one man's sin to the extent that even the animals were killed too? This seems so harsh, but looking at what happened, it appeared to be the best remedy at the time.

# CHAPTER FIVE

# When our Past Failures have Caught up with Us

In the past and today's world, no one is perfect. Even though many of us try to portray to others that we are perfect, the truth remains that none of us are. Because of our humanity, we all make mistakes. Some are just diminutive issues, while others are great and cost us a lot. Our failures can be deadly at times. Even though there are some past failures we might be able to brush off and move on, some leave scars that cause constant reminder.

As we live and do things every day, sometimes our past failures can find a way back into our lives and haunt us. While these vary in significance, the turmoil of others can bother us for a long time. For women, being pregnant at an inopportune time is something many people have had to deal with. These unwanted and unplanned pregnancies can create "inconveniences."

Thus, they can abort them without affecting their lives or missing out on some great opportunity.

The real problem starts when after so many unwanted pregnancies have been aborted, by the time they think they are ready to have children, they do not get pregnant. Most people seek medical assistance from fertility doctors and go through all kinds of procedures, but nothing seems to be work. At such a time, their souls can be overwhelmed with so much grief that not even romance can give them any satisfaction.

This is a real burden for many women today. Some women are crying in the corners, asking God where is he in their trouble – now that they are changed, and want to be serious and settle down. Even though they may seek professional help, sometimes it is in vain.

Many African families are troubled by such circumstances and usually blame the infertility on the women. Today's medical science proves that often the problem is not with the women, but it is the men. Unfortunately, because of the lack of modern technology in those areas, women unknowingly accept the blame as in-laws attack them for the lack of babies. This is so cruel.

Many who are Christians are perplexed by this. They feel that regardless of their past, once they surrendered their lives to God, he should answer all their prayers and solve their problems. To some extent, such faith in God is good and realistic. But unfortunately, I wish I could ask God why is it that some prayers are answered in the way we want, or even beyond our expectations, while other prayers are not answered at all.

The problem comes when a woman who had the abortion before her conversion, cannot bear children now and must suffer barrenness, even though she is now Christian and has asked God for forgiveness. The same issue occurs with illicit drug abusers. They have difficulties because of their drug abuse history, possibly violent gangs, and irresponsibility in their past. All of these things can come to haunt the victims, even after they have changed.

In this scenario, we see that not all Christians' prayers are answered just the way they expect. For example, there are many good single Christian women who will never marry until they die. There are many good and faithful Christian women whose past failures are making them suffer this plague of childlessness. It may look like their past failures have finally caught with them and all they can do is accept that fact, that there are times when we have to bear the penalty for our wrongdoing, no matter who we are.

Not all women seeing a fertility doctor would tell the truth about their condition, although they fully know that their lack of children could really be because of terminating unwanted pregnancies. Even though these abortions seemed appealing to them at the time, the grief they suffer for the lack of children surpasses the need to look their best and take care of important business.

Though there are many women who have already come to terms with this and accepted the consequences of their actions, they are still at the mercy of God. Then there are many who would rather be miserable and blame God and other people for their misfortune. This is a very sad and embarrassing reality. May God help our ladies.

In spite of all the things said, we know that our God is gracious and plentiful in mercy. That is why we can still come to him for forgiveness and restoration when we have sinned against him and others. We know that God has power to perform miracles beyond our expectations and that he can truly forgive our past and show us mercy, not only by just answering our prayers, but he can give us a new heart and spirit to help us make just and moral choices in our lives for the present and for the future. These new just and moral choices would bring us relief and help build a better future for us and our families.

Actually, God is truly forgiving, but that does not mean that we can defy the natural order of things as we ride on his mercy. For example, if we were heavy smokers and drinkers, just because we are now Christians and have surrendered ourselves to God does not mean that we might not die of cancer or liver problems.

Even though heavy smokers and drinkers might not die of cancer and liver problems, the risk of dying from those ailments is higher. But we can still die from those issues after we become saved. Having said that, while I do believe that our God is a loving and compassionate God, he set things in order, and by going against these commandments, we bring havoc to ourselves.

Some of us are very immoral. We may have slept around and had many illegitimate children. Now we have to deal with the remorse this brings from those kids and the other parent or families involved. Some of us have to pay alimony or child support for our children; even though we do not make much money – even if we earn enough, it is just a lot of distress to deal with constantly.

We now regret the day we met the other person who we did not really love, who bore our children. Possibly our plan of marrying the man or woman who had our first child is only a dream that was never realized.

People wonder in despair and ask God, "Where were you when we got into all this mess," or "Where are you now as we suffer the ugly past when we did not know you or really know any better."

Unfortunately, for many of us, we just have to accept the fact that our past failures have caught with us. We cannot go back to yesterday and change the way things are. All we can do is to do the best we can do for our children and families, try to rebuild our broken relationships, and enjoy the short time we have to live here on earth.

We need to pay our child support and make plans to get custody of our kids to be in their lives, and do whatever we can do now as we rekindle those broken relationships. We do not have to pretend or be ashamed forever. We must take the bull by the horns and face our human weaknesses by repairing things, so we can move on with our lives and not let our past failures undermine our current lives and the prospect for a better tomorrow.

There are some of us who have had real tragedy. It is not about paying child support or having problems with in-laws, or suffering from childlessness due to our past. It may be about attracting sexually transmitted diseases. Even though there are many of these diseases, not all of them are deadly; some can be cured.

Meanwhile, there are others for which there is no current cure, and if you became infected, you might as well make preparations for your funeral!

As far as medical science is now concerned, there is no cure for some diseases and the only advice is for each person to practice abstinence or use protection. When we go out having a good time with those who are basically strangers, in some steamy circumstances, many times we do not remember that we can possibly attract some terrible disease. It is possible that will make that sexual experience very sour, disgraceful and regrettable event forever. The sad news comes when we see immediate or gradual changes in our bodies and the really bad news may come when we visit our doctor and discover the terminal disease we have contracted.

The news of HIV/AIDS is life-altering! Even though today there are various treatments that prolong the lives of HIV/AIDS victims, there is no cure. So, attracting such a deadly disease just for having a good time in bed with a stranger, a fling, or your spouse can be devastating to hear. We can attract this incurable virus by going out with someone who is infected without any prior knowledge. Once we sleep with the person, we may fall prey to the deadly virus. But the real grief and injustice comes when an unfaithful spouse or "special someone" infects the faithful partner.

Why should the faithful partner suffer the deadly consequences of the unfaithful one? I am so sorry; I don't really have an answer, but to only say that this is not fair, and is a terrible obstacle. Even though it is possible that that unfaithful partner might not even know they have it, until sometime later when one of them sees a doctor before the bad news can be discovered.

Regardless of this, it is just not fair for the unfaithful partner to cause the other to suffer the same fate and possibly die, unless God performs a miracle. This tragedy knows no special people or group. It is not about Africans, Americans, Europeans or Australians, there are unfaithful people everywhere who bring such disasters to their faithful loved ones.

Unfortunately, this happens and it is very sad. I wonder in despair over another facet of this issue. There are many HIV/AIDS victims who have children. Even though the man and woman know their situation, they sometimes disregard counsel from their doctors and get pregnant anyway. Wait a minute – babies whose parents are HIV- positive already have the virus before they are born. Or is it possible that sometimes the unborn child does not get infected?

So, why should the parents ignore the doctors' advice and have kids knowing that the children may suffer the pains associated with the disease? I don't know, but all I can say is that this is very appalling. I would call this is slow murder that the parents commit. I think the authorities should charge them with the murders of their innocent babies if they eventually die of the disease.

The shame, guilt and embarrassment associated with HIV/AIDS is horrendous. For children to learn that that their parents are HIV/AIDS positive is a shame. Once friends and family know that someone close to them has the virus, their first reaction is not to offer their prayers and other support. It is complete detachment, rejection, neglect and distance.

Many people are afraid of being infected so they would not risk their health over moral support for the victim, even if it was a family member or close friend. That is one reason why many victims die sooner. The reaction of others toward them sometimes leads them into committing suicide or being depressed, which enhances their deterioration due to the virus and shortens the life of the victim. It would have been better to offer our prayers and moral support for these people. If we were in such a situation, would we expect loved ones to flee from us or be closer to us?

Even though there is risk involved, it would be immoral to just isolate family and friends. That would just make them loose hope in life. It could make them give up when there is a God who could truly heal them, or to allow the advance of medical science to someday bring us a cure. But while the hope for a medical cure to HIV/AIDS is far-fetched, all we can do is to offer all the support we can for the victims. This is where one can truly ask this question. "Where is God?" Where is God when a faithful and dedicated man or woman has to die of HIV/AIDS and when it was not their fault? Where is God when the children of the victims have to bear the shame and guilt this sort of thing brings to everyone?

This, I tell you, is a very dreadful thing that many families struggle with. Whether our past failures made us lose a good job with lots of incentives, a potential fulfilling relationship, or some betterment to our lives, we can do few things. We must all accept that fact that we are human and we are capable of making mistakes. When we make mistakes, regardless of their weight, we don't not have to kill ourselves through regret the rest our lives; when some things are gone, they are just gone.

We may not be able to bring back an opportunity we missed. We cannot bring back babies we killed in abortion or completely restore our health. Yet we can all learn to get over it and move on. Yesterday may never come. We may never land that great job or have the children we now want so desperately. And we may never be healed of HIV/AIDS, but all we can do is to pray to God to help us do better, regardless of our current situation.

I understand when bad things happen to us that we are not responsible for, it brings us so much anger and frustration, but we must understand that just as we are not always fair and do make mistakes at times, so it is the same with others who hurt us. Some things are not as bad as others, yet some are deadly.

We must all learn to leave the past where it is, learn from it and maximize every opportunity we have today. I know it is not really fair when certain things happen, but some of the things are beyond our control. All we can do is ask God to give us grace to move, even though we still question God's whereabouts. I would like to discuss the Bible story of King David with you. King David became a powerful and rich monarch, but the many wives he had did not satisfy him sexually. As the result of this, King David, while wandering on the roof of his palace one day saw a beautiful lady taking a shower and decided that he wanted to have her as one is his concubines.

As the story goes, this lady, later known as Bathsheba, was married to one of King David's loyal soldiers. Regardless of that, he still wanted her anyway. When King David had an affair with Bathsheba, she got pregnant. Whoops, now he has to plan a grand cover-up because the Law of Moses states that an adulterous woman must be stoned to death. King David had to find a way to brutally abuse his power as King of Israel to protect his name and save his new girlfriend.

In so doing, King David plotted to cover up the problem by calling the soldier from the battlefront to come home and spend some time with his wife. When the soldier refused to sleep at home with his wife, but slept on guard in front of King David's palace, David became really angry and put together a scheme that would kill the soldier in battle so he could marry his wife. Even though David thought everything was settled and he could have his soldier's wife, it was not so. All was well with David until the prophet of the Lord confronted and punished his household for his wrongdoing. Here is the account:

[17] One evening David got up from his bed and walked around on the roof of the palace. From the roof he saw a woman bathing. The woman was very beautiful, and David sent someone to find out about her. The man said, "Isn't this Bathsheba, the daughter of Eliam and the wife of

Uriah the Hittite?" Then David sent messengers to get her. She came to him, and he slept with her. (She had purified herself from her uncleanness.) Then she went back home. The woman conceived and sent word to David, saying, "I am pregnant." So David sent this word to Joab: "Send me Uriah the Hittite." Then David said to Uriah, "Go down to your house and wash your feet." So Uriah left the palace, and a gift from the King was sent for him. But Uriah slept at the entrance of the palace and did not go down to his house.

Then David said to him, "Stay here one more day, and tomorrow I will send you back." So Uriah remained in Jerusalem that day and the next. At David's invitation, he ate and drank with him, and David made him drunk. But in the evening, Uriah went out to sleep on his mat among his master's servants; he did not go home.

In the morning, David wrote a letter to Joab and sent it with Uriah. In it he wrote, "Put Uriah in the front line where the fighting is fiercest. Then withdraw from him so he will be struck down and die." So while Joab had the city under siege, he put Uriah at a place where he knew the strongest defenders were.

When the men of the city came out and fought against Joab, some of the men in David's army fell; moreover, Uriah the Hittite died. When Uriah's wife heard that her husband was dead, she mourned for him. After the time of mourning was over, David had her brought to his house, and she became his wife and bore him a son. But the thing David had done displeased the LORD. The LORD sent Nathan to David. Then Nathan said to David, "You are the man! This is what the LORD, the God of Israel, says: 'I anointed you king over Israel, and I delivered you from the hand of Saul. I gave your master's house to you, and your master's wives into your arms. I gave you the house of Israel and Judah.

And if all this had been too little, I would have given you even more. Why did you despise the word of the LORD by doing what is evil in his eyes? You struck down Uriah the Hittite with the sword and took his wife to be your own. You killed him with the sword of the Ammonites. Now, therefore, the sword will never depart from your house, because you despised me and took the wife of Uriah the Hittite to be your own.' This is what the LORD says: 'Out of your own household I am going to bring calamity upon you. Before your very eyes I will take your wives and give them to one who is close to you, and he will lie with your wives in broad daylight. You did it in secret, but I will do this thing in broad daylight before all Israel.'"

Then David said to Nathan, "I have sinned against the LORD." Nathan replied, "The LORD has taken away your sin. You are not going to die. But because by doing this you have made the enemies of the LORD show utter contempt, the son born to you will die."

David's trouble began shortly after his ordeal with the Prophet Nathan. The first thing that happened to David was the death of the child Bathsheba bore for him. Even though David prayed and asked for forgiveness, the child died anyway.

The second thing was the case of incest. David's son, Ammon, slept with his half-sister Tamar, who was also the sister of Absalom. In revenge, Absalom killed his brother, Ammon, because he felt that his dad had not done anything to punish his brother for the shame and disgrace he brought upon the family. It was especially worrisome because of the humiliation his sister, the princess, would suffer as a woman who was raped by her brother in the king's palace.

After Absalom killed Ammon, he fled to a nearby city for three years while his father longed to see him every day. This was the third thing that happened to David. As we can see, David's troubles were intensifying. His son raped his daughter, and the other son killed that brother in revenge and fled from his father for years. David started to pay for the evil he had done by sleeping with Uriah's wife, Bathsheba, even though Uriah was a good soldier for him.

Now the fifth punishment came to the king. David was tricked and he restored Absalom before discovering it. Since he was King, he could not go back on his words. He was then forced to accept his son to live in Jerusalem with him, though in a different house.

As the sixth punishment, Absalom started a conspiracy among the tribes of Israel undermining the government of his father, King David. Before David discovered this, it was already too late. David's household was divided against itself; this was only the beginning of more trouble to come.

Absalom won the hearts of the people by telling them only if he were appointed judge of the land, he would have representatives from every tribe as part of his government to cater to the needs of the people. This was something David was not doing well. Absalom's plan was to use the city of Hebron, where most of his supporters lived, to proclaim him leader of Israel.

In his conspiracy, Absalom fooled David to let him go to fulfill a vow, which was actually to oust David from power, unknowingly to the king. Things turn out as Absalom predicted, David allowed him to go to Hebron where the people appointed him judge, which actually meant that he was the new King of Israel, even though his father, David, still held the throne.

When David heard about all of this from the people of Israel who were with his son Absalom, he fled from his palace and became displaced. David and his envoy cried like little babies, from fear that Absalom would find them and overpower them because he had more men with him. From Hebron, after his inauguration, Absalom took his army straight to the palace in Jerusalem to fight his dad.

Fortunately for David, he was already on the run. So, the conspiracy succeeded. Absalom scared David off his throne and the King fled for his life in disgrace, even traveling barefoot. When Absalom searched the palace and found some of David's concubines, he stayed at the palace and slept with them. That was not good. If I was there I would have told him, "hey man, do not sleep with those women, they are your father's wives!" Ouch! Absalom slept with his father's wives! He did not care. To Absalom, if David let Ammon rape his sister and did nothing, it was no greater offense to sleep with his father's wives. What a wicked payback!

Do you think David's past failures caught up with him? Do you think he overpaid for them to some extent? I think so, but that is why we as leaders are not supposed to do certain things. I share my sympathy for David; he was running barefoot while his son was having a fi ne time with his wives. What a pity!

Let's stop for a minute. Let us again review the family history. King David committed adultery with his soldier's wife and she became pregnant. To prevent shame, David plotted and killed the soldier, and then married his wife adding to the many wives he already had. Later, his son, Ammon, raped his daughter, Tamar. When David did nothing to punish Ammon, Absalom killed his brother in revenge. Absalom fled for his life for three years, and as a way to return, he tricked his father and was restored.

After a short while, Ammon started a conspiracy and ousted David. His humiliated father fled from the throne in Jerusalem, in shame and disgrace. He and his whole envoy cried because of the embarrassment. In the end, Absalom was killed by David's men, and David was restored to the throne after much disgrace.

Let me ask a question, "Do you really think sleeping with someone's wife and murdering the husband was sin enough for this entire horrendous calamity upon King David, his household and the nation Israel? I don't think so, but when we do not control ourselves, sooner or later we can get ourselves in a big mess. I bet King David was not just crying out of shame and embarrassment, but I think he was asking, "God, where are you when I have to run for my life because of my own son? Where are you, God?"

Life is sometimes like that when our past has finally caught up with us. Certain things are just not worth it. The temporary pleasure and satisfaction we feel can have deadly consequence, like a woman with unwanted pregnancy or contracting HIV/AIDS, or in the case of King David, being disgraced by your son, of all people.

When such times come, let us not give up hope or commit suicide and just accept the result of our actions. We must accept that fact that our yester days have caught up with us.

We must ask God for forgiveness and walk in his grace toward restoration and destiny. He can transform us, transition us to higher heights that we could never have conceived of or imagined, or just given us our heart's desire. I encourage us not to give up in the face of misfortune, especially when we have brought it upon ourselves. We must all still seek the face of God. He is compassionate enough to help us, restore us, and give us a future no matter what we have done. Don't give up, keep walking the walk and talking the talk.

One day I will share a personal testimony with you about my life. It is a story of knowing the right thing to do, but refusing in it the name of temporal self-gratification. Today I have a story in my life that I am not really proud of, a story of shame, disgrace and loss. I went for pleasure, but it was short-lived, because all I ended with was suffering and some dreadful memories. I will tell it to the world someday to spread caution to the people.

# CHAPTER SIX

## When No One Wants to Serve

Today there are many people who prefer to be served rather than serve. I don't understand this phenomenon at times, but the fact remains that people just love to sit back, do nothing and enjoy. Sadly, there is no difference between those who profess to be Christians, including those who attend church regularly, and those who are not religious or active at all –there are proud people everywhere.

Many Christians who attend church regularly seem to prefer not to serve others; even right there in the congregation. As a matter of fact, they become upset when the ushers do not recognize and serve them properly. I have seen people ignore the ushers at church and other gatherings to take prestigious seats different than what the ushers offered them. They want to be seated in a place of comfort and where they can be seen or noticed.

Meanwhile, the right thing to do is to be of service to others. This service should not be gender-biased, religiously strained, politically motivated, for sexual exchange, or any other selfish ambition. We all should all serve others because it is the good and moral thing to do. When we serve others, we make them feel special and we too receive a reward for doing something good to help someone who might not otherwise get the assistance. Without any discrimination, we should serve others out of kindness.

One question quickly pops in my mind about why Christians, of all people, whose sins are forgiven because of Christ's sacrificial ministry (wherein he came down from heaven in the form of a man, served the people, died a vicarious death on the cross, and gave us freedom from his service unto mankind), yet we do not want to exhibit service in our lives? I want to know why this is so? Ah, ungrateful Christians!

Are we really that ungrateful or maybe we feel such sacrifice was only meant for Christ and not us as his followers? I don't know, but like most everyone else, some of us prefer to be served. If Christians are really "Christ-ians" – meaning Christ-like – then how can we claim to be Christ-like without living the lifestyle and service of Christ?

There is a sad but irresponsible reality in congregations when it comes to service. The ratio is about 20/80, meaning only 20% percent of all churchgoers want to serve, and that is those who are enlisted to serve, but not the individuals who actually do the work. The number is even less for those who really get out there and do something to help others in the name of the Lord. This is not right. It is a disgrace that we who have received His grace are not graceful enough to serve, so that in our service others might come to know Christ.

In the Bible the Apostle Paul challenged the Christians when he said, [18] "If you have any encouragement from being united with Christ, if any comfort from his love, if any fellowship with the Spirit, if any tenderness and compassion, then make my joy complete by being like-minded, having the same love, being one in spirit and purpose. "Do nothing out of selfish ambition or vain conceit, but in humility, and consider others better than you. Each of you should look not only to your own interests, but also to the interests of others.

Your attitude should be the same as that of Christ Jesus: who, being in very nature, God, did not consider equality with God something to be seized, but made himself nothing, taking the very nature of a servant, being made in human likeness. And being found in appearance as a man, he humbled himself and became obedient – even death on a cross! God exalted him to the highest place and gave him the name that is above every name, that at the name of Jesus Christ, every knee should bow, in heaven and on earth, and under the earth, and every tongue confess that, "Jesus Christ is Lord, to the glory of God the Father."

We can glean a few things from this passage. As Christians, we are receiving encouragement in our unity with Christ Jesus. We are enjoying his comfort, love and compassion. Then why are we not sharing such unique experiences with others through our service, so they too can be blessed? The Apostle, in this passage, does not ask for donations or offerings or anything else to enrich himself, but he challenged the believers to serve others just as Christ did, and then his joy would be made complete. He said if we are lavishly enjoying such grace, and of course, many of us could use extra grace, we in return should do the simple thing by reaching out to others as well.

I like this warning he issued quickly that in our service to others, we should not do anything out of selfish ambition (some of us do not keep our mouths shut whenever we do good). We climb all the towers and highest mountain tops to announce it to everyone, in our phone conversations, post it in online social networks, and in gossips. Some people may even say it as a "testimony" in church. Many people in need of help usually do not say it; or simply refuse help because they are simply afraid of the aftermath. It is rude and immoral to offer assistance to a needy person and then use it as a bargaining chip against the person later on, or point to it in insults during a misunderstanding.

We must learn to respect the integrity of others, regardless of their circumstances. Such things do not assist in friendships or evangelism. They create grounds for distrust for Christians and compromise evangelism. Basically, such loud-mouths complicate things for real Christians who want to serve others out of compassion and goodwill. If you are one of those doing this, or at least know someone who does, please ask God to really change you and anyone you know, because this behavior is destroying others. We must stop it.

Having lived close to the African refugee communities in Glendale and Phoenix in Arizona in the early 2000s, I have seen things that are not good regarding service. As a matter of fact, it was not service at all; is it called bait. Let me explain: as the influx of refugees continued to rise in Arizona, some African men who were well settled down began clandestine outreach to the refugee community.

Unfortunately, their interest was not really in assisting everyone. Their focus was on the women, especially the good looking ones. What a pity! They visited the low-income apartments where various humanitarian agencies such as Catholic Charities and International Rescue Committee will place the refugees, to check them out. Let me name few of the communities: Royal Palm (Royal Palm Road & 59th Ave in Glendale), 43rd (43rd & 45th Ave & Thomas Road), Freeway (I-17 & Thomas Road), Greenway (Paradise Shadows – 27th Street & Greenway Road).

Now out of all these housing areas, the most visited one was Royal Palm because lots of good looking women lived there.

Most of the people at 43rd and 45th Avenues and Thomas Road were pregnant women or women with lots of children. They were not quite the party type, so my good guys did not go there regularly. At Greenway, it was mostly elderly women. They did not make good female friends as well.

The same was true about Freeway; they didn't want to mingle much. The City of Glendale Police can well attest what sort of conditions existed at Royal Palm Apartments because they were always called there. It was turning into a mini Las Vegas, and that's why my good guys loved the place. And this is how it happened. My good guys would go there in the name of helping with the vital integration process. Newcomers accepted anything that looks like help because they were so needy.

They simply needed someone to teach them how to ride the bus, do grocery shopping, register their kids in school, go to church, connect with others and of course, find a social outing.

So my good guys would come in and offer such good intentions to help. Instead of taking the bus and missing your route, they offered to take the females.

Since their main desire was not to offer service to their fellow countrymen out of compassion and goodwill, they began asking for sexual favors. Help was delayed for those who initially refused them, and if they continued to say no, it finally stopped. It was a "nothing-for-nothing" deal. For those who caved in, the fun and regular assistance continued. As these men were sleeping with the women, some of whom were married or engaged, fights soon emerged, and that is why the Police were always present.

These so-called helpers soon began to leave their wives and stable relationships and hopped into new sexual affairs that sprouted from their ill-intended assistance and service to the refugee community. These problems, over the years, did not go away, they only intensified.

This is where I wonder, "oh God, where are you? Why did I share this story?" It is totally unbecoming for anyone to help out of selfish ambition, whether to make a name, for sexual benefit, or anything else. We should not do so.

Let us serve as Christ did. Christ was selfless, being the very nature of God He did not consider equality with God, but he chose to serve humanity. All believers should be like mindedly serve just like Christ did, even to the point of death – if it comes to that.

Meanwhile, there are many areas of service in our communities that do not threaten us in any way. As a matter of fact, the people in those communities will hail us as heroes and role models. All we need to do is find a need and fill it. I love this last part. Because Christ humbled himself to serve, God exalted him to the highest place and gave him a name that is above every name, the name Jesus Christ, and the measure of that name, all things in heaven, on earth and beneath earth listen. Things happen when that name is called.

Yes, I know we Christians know how to use his name, especially when we want something. Most of the time we do it without understanding what it takes to deserve enjoying the benefits of that name. We use the name of Jesus Christ recklessly.

I also come to understand that even non-Christians can use that name and get results. Isn't it strange that we love to enjoy the benefits of the name of Jesus Christ, but don't want to pay the sacrifice of service that comes with it? Oh my goodness, God is very merciful. Thank God that I am not God; I do not know whether I could take such nonsense.

Service is of vital importance in the church, in the business sector, in social arenas and in politics. Service really seems to move people as it touches both the intellectual and emotional wellbeing of humankind. If this is so, then why should there be a 20/80 ratio in churches when it comes to service, and why is it not being display correctly in other areas of life? I do not really understand. If service can move people, why don't we serve others, both as a duty and out of goodwill? So many good things will happen if we just decide to serve others.

Imagine a church of 5,000 people, all serving one school district, being pen-pals and reading buddies, giving much needed supplies, and tutoring students after school and assisting their parents. What a good thing that will be! Then see several high schools in a community serving the people in that area, or what would it be like if our favorite sports teams decided to help the poorest neighborhood in their city? This sort of momentum can change our communities, cities and even our nation. If we can do it, I tell you, it becomes contagious because of the advent of the internet, as people post developments about their projects online. And, before we know it, this could be international, a worldwide phenomenon!

As you know, people prefer shopping at stores or doing business with companies that have good customer service. Businesses quickly expand when they have good service. The same is true for churches and social organizations as well. I ask myself the question again, if through our service we can bring others to Christ, why is it that we Christians shy away from service? I wonder, is it because of pride, money or status?

If I were God, I would say to myself, "is it just because I bless them and now they have things, and connections, they feel too good and do not want to carry on my mission by helping others in desperate need?" Now you know where I am coming from. If

I were God, I would take away all of the things that make people feel this sort of arrogance. Why is it that many of us when others have helped us, find it difficult to help others? Isn't this supposed to bereciprocal at least? I think this simple way could help some of us to start. We could see it as, I help you today, you help someone tomorrow, or help me when I need it. It is simple as that, right?

But we make simple things complicated, and then suffer the consequences. I pray that God will help us change such bad behaviors.

Where is God? This question comes into my mind when I see others enjoy, and yet they do not want to share just a little with the needy, and they do not want to serve anyone at all. Some of us are more blessed than others. We should be good enough to share with others or at least serve our communities, especially those in great need. As we do this, we will establish an army of volunteers from the corporate world to the small businesses, and on to groups and individuals. This new fascination will be so contagious that sports clubs and religious leaders, as well as politicians, would just have to join. Such momentum would be passed on to schools and community leaders who will also challenge their communities to do the same, by reaching out and serving others.

I'll tell you the truth. Both the volunteers and the beneficiaries would feel good because such good deeds are reciprocal. This is really a noble and moral thing to do. I challenge you and all your friends to do something today to serve others. You could be the answer to someone's prayers. And if you do, I believe and I can guarantee you that only good things will happen. Now, go and serve others just like Christ Jesus served humanity.

There is a model of evangelism that I love because it is all about humility and service. The thrust of the program is all about rendering human services and building capacity. It combines evangelism with community development. This model was invented by a veteran missionary who lives in Arizona. It is called CHE, "Community Health Evangelism" or "Community Health Education." CHE is a worldwide phenomenon; it is in Africa, Asia, India, Europe and many other parts of the globe, transforming people and places.

CHE runs in four different ways just to be of service to people depending on the community and social strata. It can be run through government agencies, life, health and social welfare, churches, community, and through families. There is a joint venture of church and community called church initiated CHE. The operation of the CHE program is fine tuned to bring development and encouragement to people.

Even though CHE is in many places, some churches or religious entities reject or play down CHE and its development, for fear of changing traditions or loosing relevance, thereby accepting to keep their communities down so that whatever they do can be seen and praised by the people, although with little or no tangible effects or long term solutions.

Helping people the wrong way is as precarious as not helping at all. There are times when the help given to people in crisis can worsen their situations. When it comes to rendering services to people, we must all check our motives first and then examine our operations to see how much of what we can do will truly benefit the people. It is good to help others, but having good motives and accomplishing them correctly is far better.

I want to encourage you today to find a way to be of service. You do not have to start a humanitarian organization or spend thousands of dollars in order to be helpful. If you are capable of doing so, that's fine, but I believe each of us in our own capacity or within a group can bring lasting solutions to people and communities in need.

Do not sit back and expect someone else, or some agency or government to do something. If you are in a position that you can be a blessing to someone, be charitable and benevolent. The American government believes so much in helping suffering people that within its tax system are codes employed to give tax exemptions to people and organizations that give to charity. So what are you waiting for? Do not shy away from giving. It is no embarrassment to identify with some cause or people, and you will be glad you did. Be a hero today!

# PART 2
# FAMILY PEOPLE

In this section I discussed the delicate issue about infertility and abortion. While others are praying to God for babies and paying for expensive medical procedures to have babies, yet others are killing them in abortion. I wish there was a way to trade places. Sickness can make us ask tough questions about God, friends and family. It involves money and a lot of care. Sadly
at times in our pain we are neglected, abandoned and taken advantage of. This does not have to be so.

Death is a terrible thing. Nobody wants to die without enjoying life to the fullest. People died many times untimely deaths and very terrible deaths. Death brings money problems, family feuds and sometimes suffering upon those left behind. It is not fair. I bring up these tough and sometimes controversial issues because we need God to show up in them. I pray you will gain
insight as you read it. Thank you.

# CHAPTER SEVEN

# When Infertility and Abortions Abound

There are some things that are difficult to talk about. The issue of infertility (not being able to get pregnant) is a serious and sensitive issue. Many couples, especially married women and those in serious relationships, cry daily for help or divine intervention just to get pregnant. Some women go from doctor to doctor, church to church, prayer center to prayer center, and even to herbalists for this issue, to no avail.

The sad thing about infertility is that while many loving couples struggle so hard to get pregnant, some women resort to abortion. They see their embryos or unborn babies as "unwanted pregnancies," an "embarrassing thing" or a "life delaying situation." They get pregnant recklessly only to terminate, because they say they are not ready. In spite of the fact that there are so many contraceptives available, including free condoms, many women get pregnant and then destroy the baby growing inside them. Some women have multiple abortions every year when good couples are suffering in their desire to have babies.

Many times it is the middle class and poor who suffer from this problem. At least the upper class and affluent, can use medical means such as fertility procedures or surrogates as options. The necessary "items" from the man and woman can be extracted and cultured, and later inserted into the woman for further development. Even though this is costly, for those who can afford it, it is a unique science and solution to settle their problem.

The issue of infertility in West African countries like Liberia, Nigeria, Ghana or La Cote d'Ivoire can be very bad. The same is true in many other places around the world, but as we have seen in West Africa, it creates unnecessary family feuds to the extent that relationships and family ties can be broken.

In such places, people assume the infertility issue is solely the woman's fault without seeking medical attention to discover the source and how to deal with it. Men in these relationships can subject the women to both physical and verbal abuse. There are times that they will withhold support and even food occasionally, just to punish the women for not bearing babies. For some men, it gives them reason to have multiple wives or partners.

In-laws, most especially mothers-in-law, can be so rude and wicked to their sons' wives or fiancés for not being able to get pregnant. As a matter of fact, some mothers-in-law goes to the extent of throwing their sons' wives out of their own matrimonial homes!

Ill-informed, rude and arrogant mothers who think their sons' wives are eating their food, living in decent homes and enjoying all the luxury of the sons' hard-earned money without any benefit to the family. As far as they are concerned, children are the only benefit to the family, whereas their sons' happiness and the company the ladies provide to their sons are irrelevant. What a travesty!

Quite interestingly, in many poor countries, women are always blamed for not being able to procreate. But I am led to ask, are the women supposed to get themselves pregnant, or biologically speaking, is it not the men who are to share in taking care of that business? Why do people that wicked? I wonder why these uneducated people do not think that the men's sperm could malfunction or insufficient, to cause this issue. There could be complications in the reproductive system of the men that inhibit pregnancy. Perhaps the guys are shooting blanks; it could be low sperm count or bad sperm.

Infertility can come from many places. There are reports that couples, after their flamboyant weddings, are not able to consummate the marriage. Simply put, the couples are not able to have sex and they do not have sex. It can be both physiological and psychological.

People from all backgrounds or good upbringing can fall victim. This is also common among people from harsh religious backgrounds. When boys and girls in their early age are taught chastity thoroughly, when they are trained or coerced to deprive themselves of sexual emotions, by the time they are grown up, maturing out of that lifestyle to become "normal" married couples may cause a problem.

When that is the case, the couple, not just one person, needs counseling and medical attention to release tension, to learn to support each other and create sexual arousal. They must be there for each other in order to keep their relationship going in spite of the problem. They must devise ways to make each other comfortable in the bedroom. It takes the two to make it work.

Some couples do have sex regularly. But their sexual behaviors do not result in pregnancy. The women could be taking contraceptives, or the men physically remove themselves during climax to avoid the union of the seed and the egg - without which pregnancy cannot be achieved. When couples do this, it will be difficult, if not impossible, for them to get pregnant. We need to ask the couple of their sexual behavior if it supports pregnancy; this could be the problem.

When this bareness happens, many of women cry out in despair saying, "oh God, where are you?" This cry comes from the anguish deep within their souls for rescue. There are many injustices committed against women, but the plight of infertility is a very personal one that can damage a woman's soul.

With in-laws on the one side insulting or ready to kick the women out, men have extra marital affairs to give them children, friends mock them, or whatever the situation women face about infertility, we must listen to their cry. It is my prayer and hope that women everywhere who face this problem will take courage in the Lord.

It would be a more honorable thing when men come to the understanding that, although some women became reckless with bad abortions or some other physical trauma as the reason for their infertility, to realize that the problem could be the men. Whatever the case may be, I implore all men everywhere to love their women because love conquers all things. With or without children, let love conquer all things. Real men should love their women and not lay out conditions that make love impossible. It is about love and not a contract for procreation.

For men who feel they must have children, I think it is wise to seek a medical checkup for any possible infertility issues before taking the hands of the ladies in marriage, lest they and their families start berating the women for not having children. For the men who must have kids to be happy, they should spare themselves the trouble and do their private investigation to avoid the misery.

I pray for women everywhere who are caught up in this mess to take courage. It would be better for some women to leave the relationship than to endure physical and emotional abuse from the men and their families. For other women, hard work, prayer, medication and attention is quite necessary. It would take patience and you will win the battle. One day God may give you your own children. Take heart.

# CHAPTER EIGHT

# When Sickness Strikes

Sickness, whether terminal or not, is something that no one wants. I do not think anyone in their right mind wakes up in the morning and say, "ah, today I feel like being sick, especially sickness that will cause me to suffer or kill me." No, normal people do not do that. Illness is an unfortunate part of life. For many reasons the human body can break down and not function properly. Some sicknesses come because of the environment, others because of heredity, some because of a life event, or at times, the human body just begins to malfunction. Whatever the cause of the illness, it is does not any way diminish the pain it can cause.

I hate sickness. I think everyone should hate it also, and work together in unison to promote healthy communities by eliminating the human causes of sickness and find new ways to prevent and cure all illnesses.

### a. Corporate Wickedness in the Health Industry:

Before I talk about the problems illnesses creates for which we cry to God for help, let me be quick to say, there are entities who want masses of people to get sick and remain sick so they can cash in on medical services and products to the suffering and death of many. This is travesty and sheer wickedness. Sadly, the truth is that some pharmaceutical companies, hospitals and medical professionals propagate these evils in our neighborhoods every day.

Instead of finding cure to sicknesses in medicine, tools and services, many of them invent ways to maintain our illness so we do not die early, but prolong our state of bad health so they can "treat" us, as they provide medical services and products to maintain the illness for some time, instead of curing the maladies.

Some health-related companies and professionals offer services and products that are similar to placebos that do not help in our quest to better health. They just find ways to keep us alive, maintain us and make few bucks before we die. Some medical doctors give patients unnecessary surgeries and medications that are not all that relevant to healing them. They do this most of the time when the patient has cash to pay or good insurance coverage. Even doctors, of all people, want to cash in on their patients.

Although the health business is a billion-dollar industry, some engage in foul play to collect even more cash at our demise. This is not to say that some pharmaceutical companies are not trying hard to develop medicines to cure sicknesses, neither is it to say that some medical companies are not inventing tools to enhance medical procedures and that some doctors are not working tirelessly to save lives.

### b. Corporate Responsibility in Health Industry:

On the contrary, there are reputable pharmaceutical companies and professionals in the health industry that make huge profits while they provide goods and services with the patients at the heart of their intentions. As a matter of fact, some corporations and professionals in the health industry want to be first to invent the new drug or new tools to help cure terminal diseases like cancer, high blood pressure, HIV/AIDs, etc.

Their ultimate goal is to champion the next drug, vaccine, and/or medical equipment that will cure major diseases. Some run competition to provide the next beauty or weight loss supplement or procedure to help people. Whether it is finding ways to heal STDs, hereditary diseases, birth defects or strange abnormalities, corporations and professionals work around the clock in good competition to benefit the sick and prevent illness.

In this light, everyone wins. The professionals and corporations win because they champion some new item or service that people want because it is working. They can take pride in their invention and we can hail them and consult them at ease. We, the people, win because the new invention can help us take care of the sick and prevent illness. This is how it should be, and what corporate responsibility is all about – making profit yet benefitting people.

### c. Justice and Health Industry:

If you are in a country where the justice system and the health industry are in bed with each other, then you do not have anyone to speak on your behalf. This is tragedy. In some countries, whatever the doctor does or says is final, like in my country, Liberia. Untrained doctors are killing patients every day.

There is no one or any system to hold the medical professions and health corporations accountable for anything. If you are in a place like this, my friend, only God can help you, even in the western world where they can be brought to the book, there are lots of hoops to jump through, then how much more it is for countries where patients suffer and die because of bad medical practices or bad drug or equipment?

While it is difficult for the justice systems to spot and apprehend these people and companies, it is our prayers that society will frown on these things and level harsh punishments to serve as deterrents. It is our hope that the justice systems will not take bribes and circumvent laws to benefit their clients but to stand up for justice for humankind. We understand we must pay for health related services and products one way or the other, but it is not fair for some people and companies to treat us as mere numbers in their profit-making saga without conscience.

### d. Sickness brings Pain and Anger:

Sickness brings pain, anguish, frustration, family problems, financial problems, abandonment, neglect and anger. In sickness, especially prolonged sicknesses, it is easy for people to question God and their religious beliefs. They wonder why the good and loving God will allow sickness to befall them.

They get frustrated why they do not get healed after all the prayers, fasting, and religious duties are performed to no avail. This frustration causes some people to question the integrity of God and his ability to save. Others want to confront God and tell him that it is not fair; some people just cry out in anguish and ask God "why me?"

When people are sick, even the testimony about other people's healing and miracles can make them jealous and angry. They tell God in their hearts that it is not good that he takes care of others but forgot about them when all of us are his children. Some people see it as favoritism and discrimination. When people get in such an angry state, many of them come to hate God for not helping them. Christianity has lost a lot of people to sicknesses because they feel that God did want to heal them. As a matter of fact, many people today are not Christians and do not want to become Christians because God did heal their family, friend, or loved one. All they are left with is the painful memory of the suffering and anguish of the sick.

It is easier to spot those who really do not care about us in our time of trouble or sickness. People who do not care see our illness as a waste of time and resources. They complain about hospital visits, our absence, and even the concern and sympathy others show for us.

### e. Abandonment and Neglect in Sickness:

Many people's health deteriorates because of abandonment and neglect. They get so frustrated with family and friends who forgot them. Sadly, this increases the illness. When you visit hospitals and see patients that have been there for a month or more, it is easier to understand this.

Meanwhile, patients in the hospitals who have no one to visit them seemed to be better off than their counterparts who are old and or disabled in group homes or nursing homes.

It can be so terrible that people who were the shakers and movers of society end up in a place where the only people they see regularly are the nurses that care for them. Family and friends many times forget about them. They can become so lonely to the extent that some of them wish for death daily.

If family members do visit them, it is usually on holidays like Thanksgiving or

Christmas. But when they are approaching death, or when they do die, even the nurses can be surprised at all the so-called family who come. Most of them who show up come to find faults with the nurses or facilities so they can file lawsuits. They come to seek opportunities to make profits out of their loved ones they did not really care about. This is an appalling thing.

While I have been talking about the sick and the frustration they face, the scene depicted suggests the Western or developed world where good medical professionals and facilities exist, but there are other places where the lack of medical professionals and modern medical facilities become the first issue.

## f. Illness: Lack of Good Doctors and Hospitals

Being sick is one thing, but being sick in a place where there is no doctor or good doctor, or good hospital and other medical facilities, increases the death rate of the ill. It actually creates hopelessness; hope is something that is vital to the healing process. To all of our brothers and sisters in the undeveloped world where there are no doctors or well-trained medical practitioners and well-equipped medical facilities, I am so sorry. As the many of you have put your trust above the existing systems which are ill-equipped to help you, I pray that God will give you faith and help you in your time of illness.

I greatly encourage you to put your trust in God for your healing, for He can take care of you beyond what any doctor can do. Trust the Lord and do all you can to stay healthy. In my short life I have seen how illness can change, deform, destroy, and finally kill people. While there is nothing good about sickness, and inasmuch as I hate it, if I am sick, I'd rather have a short-term illness that I am healed from or die from than to be sick for a long time.

Interestingly, in sickness we do not have a choice about the type and duration of the illness that come. Sickness can come with or without warnings. Either way, our bodies can break down and we suffer through aches and pains.

## g. Being Bewitched by Sickness

In talking about the origin of illness, I want to insert one aspect about its origin that many people, especially Westerners, would want to debate. Whether Westerners and other people in the civilized world agree or not, some people possess evil powers and can bewitch others with spells and charms to make them sick.

I am quite aware of science and the debate we can all make to refute my recent claims, but beyond all science and physical realities, is the supernatural that cannot be explained in our fact-finding data. I understand the misconceptions and denial of some, but just because someone does not understand a thing or phenomenon, it does not eliminate the possibility of its existence or impact.

For example, Christians and all religious people believe that God made the universe as we know it, and beyond. Science on the other hand claims that all things came into existence by chance and certain interactions of chemicals and elements over millions of years. I am aware that if a Christian does not have an answer to any question, he or she can state that God did it without further explanation.

In the same way, scientists, when confronted with some unexplained phenomena, can say that it happened by chance, interactions of the elements over time. So on both sides, even though one may claim to be right and it seems popular over the other, they are essentially expressing "faith" in different terms.

The issue of witchcraft, voodoo, spells and charms is the same. While we may give scientific explanations to anything, especially the symptoms and effects in medical terms, the truth is that these disputable and complex things are real. Have you ever heard of voodoo dolls? If you know about them, you will understand what I am talking about. For those of you who do not accept the supernatural and term it as false, unreal, hallucination or some mental illness, let me help you understand. Though I know that to some of you, due to your exposure to your own culture and environment, and because you have not seen or perhaps heard anything like this, it may seem too farfetched for you.

In many places in Africa and other places around the world, casting spells and bewitching people is a common practice that can affect many. Communities remain in abject poverty because of witchcraft and all sorts of evil practices. These people possess supernatural power to cause weather catastrophes, and can control plants and animals, as well as people.

In Maryland County, Liberia – West Africa, when the natives do their traditional dances, at times to show off, they can chop off a man's head, put it on a platter from morning until evening and then put it back on his body, and the dead man rises back to life. Yes, they can actually do that! I do not know how science can explain it, but it is true.

I brought this up because if someone is sick because he or she is bewitched, no hospital or doctor can help. Their chance of survival rests in seeking the face of God in prayers. In this light, prayer is the only medicine, church is the hospital, Dr. Jesus Christ is the best doctor to call on. This is not to say that if you are in Africa or some other place where there are witchcrafts and where there are not good hospitals and doctors, then do not seek medical treatment. No, not at all. I suggest you use all medical services available as you trust God to help you. Also, just because people are in the modern world, it does not exclude them from attacks by wicked people that cast spells, charms or practice witchcraft and voodoo.

### h. Mental Impact of Illness:

When we get sick, no matter what the source, curable or incurable, it can affect our lives. Some people can get revelations from their sick beds and begin to move forward in life while others remain in negativity thereafter. We can even experience near-death experiences that can impact our lives in strange ways with memories of the unusual things seen. Some people develop mental illness after they experience some terrible illness.

### i. There is Hope in Sickness:

Whatever the case is for the health industry and its impact on the sick, all things considered, let us pray to God and seek all available medical services for prevention and cure. I do believe there are good people and organizations out there that can help us to improve our health and assist in providing better health-related services.

The plight of the sick is relevant. The pain is real. The impact is abysmal. Yet I encourage you to stay strong, keep your heads high and believe in better days ahead. I do believe some way somehow, with God, the advance of medical science, and the benevolence of good people and organizations, we will get better health-related services and products during our time of illness. There is hope. When you are sick, please do not give up on yourself. To all of those who have sick family members, please do not give up on them in their illness. During these times, they need the support of friends and family. Keep the faith. Hold onto each other. God will help you.

# CHAPTER NINE

# When Death Comes

Death is a sad reality of life. Even though we know that we are not going to live forever, we fear death. For many of us, anytime is too soon for death. If it was left to us, we would not die. We want to live and see our grandchildren and their children's children. In short, we do not want to die. Whether we have a good reason to live or something valuable to offer, we want to continue to live. When death comes, it makes us to wonder about life itself. Dealing with death tests our resolve to live.

### a. Fear of Death

It is seldom that people celebrate the coming of death with parties and exchanges of gifts as in weddings and newborn babies. For the most part, it is not only the dying that are afraid of death, but friends, family, loved ones also become afraid. It is the coming of death of a few loving people that we can accept the situation to freely allow death to take them away. But if we could, we would resist death altogether.

The people for whom we somehow welcome death to end their suffering, we can still have some fear that when they are taken, they are gone forever and knowing that makes us scared. To know that we cannot communicate with them or interact anymore in itself is quite frightening.

There is a fear factor about death. The fear of death is without discrimination as to race, color, ethnicity, age, or social and economic status. When death is coming, everyone becomes fearful.

It appears that we are more afraid of dying than death itself.

When a family member is terminally ill, we become frightened of losing them. When our loved ones undergo serious medical procedures, we become impatient to hear from the doctors about their condition. Even though we are very curious, the truth is our curiosity is fueled by our fear to hear unwanted news – the news of death.

When we hear about an accident in a place we know friends and family are, before knowing about their safety, we get scared and hope that they are safe from tragic events. There is hope in conjunction with our fear of hearing bad news about them. The silence we feel until we hear from them can be crippling. The fact that we do not know whether they are safe can become frustrating and frightening and can really put us on edge.

In a way, death makes some people show they care when they did not do it while their friend or relative was around. Whether it is done out of guilt or sympathy, they come to offer condolences and support. Death, oh death, you are fearful!

### b. Dealing with Death

There are books and TV shows about 1,000 ways to die. The cause of death is without number. People die every day from different causes. Illness, suicide, accidents, murder, old age, poison, prenatal death, bombs, and sheer stupidity are some of the ways death approaches.

There are some people who suffer a lot from pain in sickness, an accident, or from torture before they die. I feel for them. My heart goes to people who see their family members suffer painful prolonged deaths. It is so difficult to deal with. I would rather die quickly than to suffer for a long time before I die. I thank God for all of you who stay with your family and friends in their sickness until they die. At least your company while they are going through this gave peace and comfort; it kept them from loneliness.

I have seen and heard about some people who die peacefully. They tell people that they will soon go and gave their last wishes before they gave up the ghost. Such a thing is so beautiful. My grandma told me of a man who called all of his family one day and told them that he would die soon. After giving them his last words, he began to sing songs and worship the Lord.

Some of the family members were confused, while others wept though he forbade not to cry. The next morning, he called in his wife and said farewell and died as he sang and smiled.

That was a wonderful way to die! I wish that was the way we all could pass away. Well, I guess it is not up to us to plan the way we die; it is up to God. If we try to kill ourselves or another, it would be called suicide or assisted murder.

Death brings pain. Whether it was peaceful or painful, it has a way of bringing pain to everyone. The mere absence of the dead creates problems in itself. Death can make us lose friends and family to eternity, a no-return destiny. I have seen people wail and cry so hard during death that it made me sorrowful because it was just so hard. They cried hopelessly as if there is no life for the family after the death of their friend or loved one.

What hurts about death is that sometimes the one who died was the breadwinner for the family, or the most promising person in the family. There are times people die and it can be so unbelievable because of our recent interactions with them. Death has created a lot of widows and countless orphans, without help. Many times after the burial, people seem to forget about the immediate family. Such deaths can be very devastating.

Another thing I have seen during the death of a person is

hypocrisy. Some family and friends who did not care come and act as if they do. There are times such people make empty promises during family visitations, wake-keeping and funeral services. People can be so pathetic and heartless in telling lies over the coffin of the dead and to the bereaved family.

I have also seen terrible family feuds, fights and cursing during such times. Instead of family mourning the loss and being there for each other, fights erupt and things get out of control. Some people can be so concerned about obtaining the deceased's property that they do not even wait for the burial and they want to know about the will.

One thing I pray to God about is to grant me life again for a brief moment during my funeral service so I can listen to all those who will come and lie over my coffin. Many people usually lie about things the dead did not do during their lifetime. For some reason I do not know, some feel they must say something good about the dead, even if the dead was not a good person at all.

That is why I will instruct my family to have an open coffin so I can grab anyone by the neck that comes in and lies, and pull them in during the last viewing. I have known some people who were corrupt, but during the wake and funeral services, friends and family can frame the wicked as good. I hate that and do not think it is good to lie about the dead, even if one is doing it to keep the face of the family. I believe there are better ways to state things to the bereaved family and not be offensive than saying someone was good when they have been corrupt during their lives.

There are times people died because someone murdered or bewitched them. In many places, even the ones who murder the dead come to the funeral services pretending to me sympathetic toward the family. This is cruel. They come laying flowers on the coffin like every other person knowing that they are the evil doers. It makes me to ask, "oh God where are you?" I pray that the time will come when God will reveal all of the evildoers and judge them.

Another thing that gets to me is family and friends who are in the position to help, but do not help when the dead person became sick. Thank God for the Western countries where there is medical insurances to cover the medical expenses. In places like Africa and many others around the world where there is no medical insurance, this problem is real.

It is in places like these where family and friends have to stand up for each other in sickness, but when such times, some refuse to help. When death comes, they come around pretending to be loving family or friends when they know quite well that their assistance could have saved the person. Oh God, have mercy. When all of the funeral rites are performed and the deceased is laid to rest, the frustration and pain comes because of the emptiness death creates. The role that person used to play now becomes vacant. The wife now becomes a widow, the husband a widower, the children become orphans. When the breadwinner is gone, suffering comes to the family. It is during such times the family really needs help I pray that God will help grieving families everywhere and fill the gap death creates.

Death is painful, brings sorrow, and death can cause family feud, quarrels and fights. Death brings financial problems and loneliness. I pray for families experiencing death issues that

God will console you one by one. In your times of loss, may the Almighty God be with you. In the moment of your need, may God give you hope beyond your situation, and beyond any comfort and consolation man may give, may God give you peace.

May God give you sustenance and longevity to live and testify to the goodness of God. Do not give up. Do not give in and let your situation dictate your destiny. You can pick up the broken pieces and have a full life even after such great misfortune. It may seem hopeless, please do not lose heart. Remember, even though your situation is peculiar, you are not alone in this. You are not the first, neither will you be the last, to lose a friend or family member to the cold clutches of death. Others suffered a great deal, but they did not die. They learned from the pains. They gathered themselves up and have learned to move on. I encourage you today, please take heart and move on. God bless.

# PART 3
# PERSONAL

Loneliness and hopelessness are things that can really eat us on the inside without others knowing at times. We get lonely due to lack of people and things and we get lonely in the middle of people and things when we do not fi t it. Either way, the pain can have catastrophic results if not taking care of properly.

Loss of hope is quite terrible. Hopelessness makes us stop thinking forward and we turn inward toward depression and possibly suicide. We feel that life is without meaning and the best thing to do to free ourselves is to die. This sought of distraught thinking have cause a huge loss for lots of families around the world.

I pray that all lonely and hopeless people will find comfort and hope. I challenge all of us to be mindful of those around us and learn the symptoms of these two dangerous diseases before they take our loved ones. Be the help they need. Thank you.

# CHAPTER TEN

## When Loneliness Comes

Loneliness is a ruthless sickness. It hurts people. Most of the time when we think about someone being lonely, it is easy to think about single men and women, single parents, orphans and widows. The truth is that there are many lonely people than we realize. While it is true that many single people, widows and orphans can be lonely, there are those who have people and things in their lives, but can be so lonely. There are two types of loneliness I want to discuss here.

The commonly known loneliness is caused by the absence of things and people. It is often attributed to the poor, singles, widows and orphans, because they do not have what and who they need. Unlike people in this category, there is another form of loneliness that people experience which does not come from the lack of people and things. There are those who become lonely while in the midst of plenty. They have the friends, family and things, yet they are lonely. They are always in the midst of others, but they can still be lonely. This sort of loneliness can easily lead to acute depression and it is difficult to detect.

People become lonely sometimes because they do not fit in among the people with whom they interact. For example, a single lady without a stable relationship may hang out with friends to shop, party and drink. They may even have a boyfriend or date like everybody else. They seem to be like everyone else, except there is a big difference. The difference is that, the others have men to call their own, but they do not have that someone special.

To cover up this loneliness, they find dates and boyfriends to soothe them and make them feel good, but yet in their heart they know the person does not belong to them. So even in the midst of shopping, eating, drinking and partying, they can become lonely because they do not fi t in with the group.

The sad news is that in our world, even Christians and religious people can experience loneliness. While it is true that all of us experience some sort of loneliness because we miss family, friends and loved ones, it is not constant like what the real lonely suffer. For us it is just temporal a brief period.

Whether loneliness comes because of the lack of things and people, or even in the midst of plenty, the truth remains that people get lonely and this can be a serious thing that can lead to other complications if not given proper attention in time. Loneliness comes also when we are disconnected from our purpose in life. We feel some sort of emptiness that may be difficult to explain, but we know that we miss something deep within our souls. The missing thing is our purpose in life and straying from it will always make our spirit and soul feel empty.

This loneliness will not stop unless we begin a search from deep within us. It can lead us to reevaluate our lives, to try to find the missing piece – our purpose. This type of loneliness can end when we begin to find out what is our purpose in life and begin to live it. When we begin to live that purpose in life, it gives us peace of mind. The peace casts away all fear and doubt. We can now excel in life. As we live in our purpose, it propels us forward to our destiny. Loneliness flees and joy settles in.

Being disconnected from God can make us lonely. Whether we are away from God because of ignorance or because of sin, we feel lonely. I think somehow it is better to be ignorant of God [by not knowing him and feel that disconnectedness, because there is special grace for that] than to know God and be disconnected from his fulfilling presence because of sin.

When we sin against God, it separates us from God. The prophet Isaiah said it right when he declared, **[19]** "Surely the hand of the Lord is not too short to save, nor his ear too dull to hear. But your iniquities have separated you from your God; your sins have hidden his face from you."

For believers around the world, the separation of sin is the worst kind of loneliness one can feel. It is better not to have people and things and have God, than to have all the material things and not have God. Any disconnection and absence from God, even temporal, can affect a good believer negatively.

Thank God the remedy for such loneliness is available. When we face loneliness because of sin's separation, all we have to do is go to God in prayer, confess our sins, stay away from them and cling to God. Our brother John said is right when he commented on sin and repentance, **[20]** "If we confess our sins, he is faithful and just and will forgive us our sins and purify us from all unrighteousness." When we do, the Lord renews the joy of our salvation and we have full access to him and all the kingdom benefits.

Quite interestingly, having a good relationship with God can help us deal with our entire loneliness problem. Whether it comes from the absence of people and things, displacement in position or guilt of sin, God can take care of our loneliness. The Lord gives joy, peace, comfort and sweet companionship that is so satisfying that no loneliness can stand in his presence.

When we are with God, we are in good company. Loneliness can sometimes lead to depression, and if not taken care of can lead to suicide or another cause of death. It can make us feel like nobody cares about us. At times, we get overwhelmed with change and our outlook on life in general is as if life is not worth living, because there is no one to live for or interact with.

Loneliness can make us question God and ask him some real blunt and direct questions. When we get lonely, we ask God, "Where are you?" Where is your comfort? Where is your presence? Where is your companionship? All of these are vital questions for us to ask God in our loneliness. Yet in the midst of all this, I want us to remember that God promised in his word never to leave us, nor forsake us.

So we do what do when we feel abandoned and lonely? Let us trust in the word of God and believe that God is there with us. Let us ask God to come and fill the void in our life. Let God fill that empty spot in our lives because of the desire for people and nice things we think we need to enjoy life. We all need material things. We all need people with whom to share our stories, our joy, sorrow, victories and dreams.

Let's ask God to fill that void in our lives. When we ask God he will bring special people into our lives to give it meaning. May God give us the little things we need to help us live in comfort. I believe God is just and faithful to all of us. I challenge you today to trust in the Lord and he will take care of you. Instead of loneliness, may God give you good relationship.

# CHAPTER ELEVEN

## When Hope is Lost

When someone has lost hope it can be a terrible thing. There are stages of hopelessness. The impact it has on people varies depending on the situation and strength of the people. I have seen a lot of hopelessness in people who lost jobs, relationships, family, friends, or other things in life. Sometimes the situation can be so bad that some people result into committing suicide. They just want to die so their misery will be over. They do not see any way out of their problems. They lose hope in life itself because they feel that the absent thing, person or place that is troubling them has no end. They'd rather die to forget their troubles, instead of fighting for change.

When someone loses hope in life, it is so easy for them to attempt or commit suicide. A lot of people have committed suicide and left family and friends to deal with the sorrow it brings. A neighbor killed himself in Monrovia kill himself by drinking a lot of toilet cleansers because his wife refused to have sex with him. For some time, his wife had refused him in bed, but was going out to sleep with other men, some of whom he knew. One day he said that he could not bear to live any longer and see his wife, whom he loved, sleep with other men and refuse to sleep with him.

This man was an amputee. He seemed to be a nice old man who sat with us and kept our company. He always wanted me to tell him about America. He liked talking about American politics. It is no surprise that some of us who live in America are not well informed about American politics more than those who live outside of America. He enjoyed talking politics.

To quell his frustration of not being sexually intimate with his wife and the constant threat of suicide, one of his sons offered to bring him other women, including prostitutes, just to help cool down his sexual desire. He declined the offer. He told his that son he did not want other women. He wanted his wife.

Because his wife refused to have sex as they used to on that fateful day, he drank the detergents and died. He died because of sex deprivation and lost intimacy. Upon his death, all of the children blamed their mother for his death. Whether she was sorry or not, their father had died. What a pity!

Even though it was not proper, I think it would have better to listen agree with his son if he could not stand the situation and sleep with other women, even including prostitutes, than to kill himself. Do you agree? I apologize to all of the righteous and holy people, but this man would have been alive and perhaps may have repented.

It is possible his wife too would have understood her mistakes and changed but that could not happen anymore. But now that he is dead, all hope is truly lost. Our dear friend died and all possibilities of a better tomorrow were buried with him. The children grieved, suffered frustration and embarrassment because of this. A certain lady close to my office in Liberia poisoned food that she and all her children ate, and they died. In the middle of one dreadful night she woke up the kids and made some nice but poisonous rice soup. The poison killed the whole family.

I will call her Ma Betty. Ma Betty's sister who lived in America son was staying with her and the family. She survived by assistance from her sister as she cared for her nephew. A time came when the sister in the States told her of her plans to send for her son. Sometime later, all of the documents were ready for the boy to travel to his mom in the States.

It was at that time Betty felt insecure and her hope of survival was at an end. She felt if the boy left, her sister would not help anymore, and that was why she decided to poison all of them. While it was not true that the sister would be so ungrateful as to cut off communication and support after her son left, sadly Ma Betty was deceived in her thinking and lost hope. So the departure of the boy meant a terrible time in her mind, and she felt she could not handle it. She felt her life was over.

She lost hope in the sister. She lost hope in herself and any other family, friend or relative. Ma Betty lost hope in life. It is very sad that a hopeless person can determine the fate of other innocent people. It is so unfair. I think it would have been better for Ma Better to kill herself than killing the whole family; even though it is not good.

Hopelessness can make people do irrational things they would normally never do. It is a devastating thing. Do not be a victim of hopelessness. There are many people and organizations out there that can help without asking for money. It would even be better to borrow from others to settle your problem and pay them later than to do something that is fatal.

I encourage you to communicate your dissatisfaction or frustration with others rather than to let depression bring you to hopelessness before it is too late. Learn to talk it over with others. Cry out about what is going on; you never know who can help you. Communicate. Do not let people wonder in despair saying "Oh God, Oh God" or "Where is God?" over your demise. You can do something to help yourself. Put yourself together please; you will be doing yourself a great favor and everyone connected to you. You can make it.

## WHERE IS GOD?

Once there is life, there is hope; but you must apply hope accordingly. You must search and work on it. Life itself is not easy for many of us. We must all learn to make life better daily in spite of all the negative things that happen. Do not give up. Take courage. God will help you.

# PART 4
# STORIES THAT QUESTION GOD

I know that there are many people out there with stories that would bring us sorrow, move us into compassion, frustrate us, and sometimes make us angry. Some of these stories even make good Christians question the reality of God, his love and care for his people and, in fact, his power to protect his own. These stories give platform to unbelievers and atheists, and people of other religions, to make mockery of Christians and their God. Some of the stories will really break your heart, but the people who faced the situations found a way to deal with them.

Bear with me as I share with you some real heart-wrenching chapters of the lives of people in different areas. One thing I want to help you understand before you read on is that "God is!" regardless of all the evil that befalls us. It does not make God less of a god because we or people we know have had some very terrible situations that God did not show up for as we expected.

Before we go on questioning everything we know about God or try to believe about God, please consider all of the goodness of God you have been enjoying. In spite of the circumstances that makes us question the reality of God, his love, his care and his power, let us understand that in our good times and bad times, "God is!".

# CHAPTER TWELVE

## A Sister in Kenya

Sometime ago a pastor friend of mine and I were at the dining table ready to eat dinner after a very long week of fasting and prayer when his phone rang. Usually we choose not to answer when we are enjoying a meal with company, and figure we can call them back, but this time he picked up the phone and answered.

A lady called from Kenya crying and wailing loudly, and shouting, as she talked with him. The phone was not on speaker, but I could still hear her. Such loud callers only mean fire is in the hole; I said to myself. But as we all listened, what we heard from this lady in Kenya made us forget our food and become very troubled. What was her problem you may be wondering by now?

Hold on, sit back and brace yourself as I tell you. The ranting and wailing was all meaningful finding out what happened to this wonderful soul. This is what she said in anger, frustration and deep anguish. "Hello Pastor, when you preached in Kenya and I undoubtedly saw the demonstration of the power of God that healed the sick before my eyes, the blind received sight, deaf spoke and dumb heard. Your preaching brought thousands to salvation, delivered the oppressed, empowered the churches in our city, and pushed us into a higher level of prayer and manifestations began to happen. I thought God was real and able to protect his faithful people.

How come God allowed the wicked to take charge over the righteous? You know I am a devout Christian, a medical doctor who politely refused plenty of men as I waited for God to bring me my own husband. I stayed chaste and away from fornication. I have been upright before the Lord. I paid tithes every paycheck and attended services regularly. I love God and really believed in him as my personal Lord and savior.

You know all of this and there is no doubt about that. But Pastor, tell me, how can this same God who has power over spiritual wickedness, demons, witchcrafts, can heal the sick and saved many could not protect us? Look Pastor, I am dead! With AIDS this rampant in Kenya, just a few days ago on our way from the Tarry at the church, an all-night prayer session, armed robbers jumped my friend and I right before my house gate, took our possessions at gunpoint, and raped us as they laughed.

One kept guard while the other two took turns raping us in mockery. They were laughing as we were crying for help, yet no one came to help us! They raped us! I could have enjoyed sex on my own terms, and asked God to forgive me. That's what many Christians do.

But I resolved to keep my body for my husband that God would bring me. Instead of my husband, armed robbers raped my friend and me in the open, outside my house gate. If God is real, where was he?

Doesn't the Bible say that God will protect his own and keep us from danger, and especially troubles we cannot deal with? Now I doubt if God even exists? Where was God?

Where is God now? Tell me, where is God? What did I do to deserve this? Was I wrong to live for God and keep my body clean until I marry? But instead armed robbers publicly violated my friend and me physically and sexually.

As hard as it was, I had to turn down some good affluent men who just wanted me for sex with benefits, because I wanted a husband. There was one I liked very much, he was so good to me, but he was married so I didn't want to get involved. I give up on God! I gave up. I give up; not today, not tomorrow. I give up!

Pastor, those guys were so rough. They have had sizeable male endowment. It hurt so bad that I cried until I could not cry anymore. The more I cried, the more energized they became, so I stop crying and just wished I was dead so this nightmare would be over. I thought about committing suicide just to get over the pain. Why didn't I die?

You know in Kenya how people are infected with HIV, what if I am infected? And what if I am pregnant by those bastards? Do I abort or keep it to remember the ordeal? Pastor, you lied to me, God is not real I gave up, I give up!" And she began to cry out so loud that both of us forgot about the food and began to comfort her and prayed with her. This brought much sorrow to our hearts. We did our best to assure her that even though bad things happen to good people, God is sovereign and has a way to work out things for the better.

The Lord did not give us Bible stories to help in this situation. We jumped straight to our personal lives and told her about some trying times we both had; and encouraged her. I tell you the truth: some of the problems we go through are not really meant for us. God has a way to use them as a tool to minister to others in dying need. I thank God that our weakest moments in life could be meaningful to another person. Now let me ask you, if you were there to hear this sad story, what would you say to our sister?

# CHAPTER THIRTEEN

# Cry of a Women Ministry Leader

The leader of the women's ministry in a little thriving church asked her pastor, "Is this how God make me pay for my sins? I thought Jesus' blood paid for all my sins more than 2000 years ago?" He was puzzled at her question. He knew a hurricane was on the horizon as he carefully asked her to tell him the problem. This is what she said: "You know that I had a man who proposed to marry me. We were living together and taking care of things. We loved each other, at least so I thought. We were very active in church. I was leading the women in the church, even though I have a lot to learn, but I was giving God my best. Then a young girl who recently moved in town from the village came and joined the church. As the leader of the women I reached out to her. We all began to do things together.

After a short time with us, this girl became sick and we took her to the hospital. We all thought it was just a fever or something simple. We did not know that her condition was life-threatening. This young lady had no friends and family here; all she had was the church.

## WHERE IS GOD?

The doctors said she had cancer. During her three months stay in the hospital, she had no one to look after her. I was the one pastor asked to look after her and prepare food for her. I took food to the hospital many days and stayed with her.

Interestingly, when she got better and came home from the hospital, my fiancé began to help her when I couldn't. Before I knew it, he was sleeping with her. Oh men, we can't trust some of them! I confronted this young lady and asked her to leave my man alone, but that little girl, who was so humble at the hospital, lied to my face and said there was nothing going on.

It is frustrating to know that another so-called self-made prayer mother in town told that young girl to stick to my man, and she told my man to leave me because I was too old to have kids. Wow!

To my surprise, my fiancée started leaving our house in the middle of the night claiming he was going to work, while he spent half of the night to her place. Before I knew it, she got pregnant and ended up getting married. Their marriage made me so downhearted. I was so frustrated. A few days later, he came back, packed up his stuff, and left. I was so angry. I was quite surprised and completely speechless! As a leader, I tried to hold it in and not let the women know how much I was hurting. I cried day and night when I was alone, asking where God is his justice? At some point, I put myself together and tried to move on.

Now tell me, just because I sinned before against God, does it mean that God has to punish me this way? Where is God in his mercy, total forgiveness and restoration? Where is God when a young girl stole my man? Does this so-called prayer mother go free after messing up my life? What crime did I commit that is so great that the grace of God cannot conquer?"

Wow, what a tragedy! I was really disturbed when I heard this sad story. It was humiliating because I too am a man. As God would have it, the pastor found a way to comfort her. What am I supposed to do in such situations? What can I tell her? Her complaint is real. Where is God when a young lady she helped took her man? Is this a punishment from God? The pastor and I joined together in praying for her. Join us in prayer for our sister that the Lord will comfort her and find her a real man who will love her for who she is.

Let me ask you some quick questions. What would you say to this woman? What about this prayer mother? Have you ever been offended by a pastor, priest, prophet, apostle or prayer mother? And, where is God in all this?

# CHAPTER FOURTEEN

## Ma Phebe and Junior

Ma Phebe of Gbiso is a great woman of God from Maryland County, Liberia in West Africa. She is a native of Liberia, uneducated, but very dangerous in prayer. She prayed once and a witch, (man in Barrobo in Maryland County) turned into a groundhog. One night when the skies were clear, a witch was flying on a broom, and she commanded the witch to fly in circles. It was one of the funniest moments of my life. She told the flying witch to surrender to God by 8:00 the next morning or die by noon. By 7:30 that morning, the man she described came running into the church bringing in all his tarot cards, robes, pipes, mixed herbs and surrendered his life to God.

Ma Phebe is a woman of faith and prayer. This is a woman prayer made the earth opened up and almost swallowed a boy who vowed to kill her by his witchcraft at her mission in Gbiso. Her prayers caused fourteen witches to die in seven in days, two each day in a small Ivorian town bordering Liberia.

The birds making their nests in the trees were silenced when she spoke to them in an open town square in one Ivorian town, because she was praying outside and they were too loud.

People were brought in cars from nearby cities and towns daily for healing, and God healed all the sick. When God is ready to move, at times he sends a signal to let us know of his power and intervention.

Her ministry is known for miracles, signs and wonders, deliverance and holiness. This woman is a renowned woman of God from Liberia, not one of those self-made prayer mothers who are eager for men, and hungry for money and titles. She is a well-known anointed woman of God from the Assemblies of God Church. Her ministry has reached across Liberia, Ivory Coast and the USA.

A couple of years ago, her son-in-law shot her at pointblank in Brooklyn Center, Minnesota. Three bullets hit her. The one that could have killed her hit her from the side. If this bullet was to pierce her heart, it would have caused instant death. But the God of Abraham, Isaac and Jacob, the God of Elijah, the God of Israel, truly the God of Ma Phebe, stopped that killer bullet. Bullets usually go straight; not bending and dodging or reversing, but for Ma Phebe, that was the case.

According to the doctor's report from the nearest hospital, for some reason, that bullet did not go straight through her ribs to shatter her heart, but instead, passed between more than three ribs, not touching one. When it reached the open cavity between the ribs and the heart, the bullet miraculously reversed and came out! How could that be? The God who is the shepherd of our souls must have sent his angels to prevent death. Had it not been for God, Ma Phebe, her daughter and grandchildren would have met a violent death in one day.

At the beginning of 1988, Junior, a beloved son of Ma Phebe, became sick. She desperately prayed for God to heal him. Instead of the usual instant or gradual miracles, what came from God was quite unusual. God told her that her son would not live. She fasted and prayed for God to remember her and heal Junior, but unfortunately, with all those long sleepless nights of prayer and days of fasting, Junior died early one morning in January of 1988.

While Junior was in his sick bed, more and more people were brought in daily for prayer and God healed all of them. The fateful morning Junior died, under the anointing of the Holy Ghost, Junior woke up, walked a few hundred feet from Ma Phebe's house to the house of a paralytic woman who was lying in bed with one whole side was paralyzed. She was the wife of a businessman in Pleebo. When she became ill, the hospital could do nothing to help her and so she was brought to Gbiso for prayer.

When Junior got to that woman, he spoke like Peter and John at the temple's gate, and said, "in the name of Jesus, rise up and walk." That woman arose and began to walk immediately, jumping up and down praising God. When she started jumping, dancing and praising the Lord, Junior returned to his bed and died.

When the people saw that this paralytic woman was walking and completely healed, they joined her in a group and walked toward Ma Phebe's house to praise the Lord. When Junior was discovered dead, the others and Ma Phebe herself, began to cry as they went to the place where Ma Phebe's husband worked to tell him about his son's death. So this is what happened: one group was coming from the north of Gbiso crying over Junior's death and the others jubilating from the south praising God about the healing that just took place. There was a great noise and no one clearly understood what was going on, but when they met in the middle, there were tears of joy from the south, and tears of death from the north. Those from the north asked the group from the south, "Why are you shouting and laughing when there is news of a death. Ma Phebe's son, Junior just died"!

The woman who was healed shouted, "The boy just prayed for me and now I am healed." When she realized that he was dead, she was so shocked that she fainted on the spot. Tears of joy for the healing was sadly turned into tears of pain because of the sudden death of the one who healed her. The days that followed became a season of some unusual accounts of the power of God. When the anointing came upon Ma Phebe, she would just stretch out her hand and the sick would receive their healing. Moreover, God spoke to Ma Phebe not to cry for her son, the son for which she had cried and prayed day and night that God would heal him, yet he died anyway.

The day Junior was buried, God spoke through another person during the morning worship service that Ma Phebe should not cry for her son at the burial. If I was Ma Phebe, I would have told God, "you are not serious. What do you want from me now? God, are you kidding me? You allowed my son to die, and now I should not cry for him at the gravesite?"

As difficult as it was, Ma Phebe held her breath and did not cry. In the midst of the pastors and hundreds of people that came from all over, Ma Phebe obeyed God and did not cry. What a thing to see! To those young in the ministry of God, I want to tell you that it is not easy to serve God so take God seriously.

By the time we returned from the grave, three cars arrived from Pleebo with many sick people who came to see Ma Phebe for her healing prayers. Now picture this, a powerful woman of God who lost her son, the son she could not cry for during his burial, just returned from the gravesite, and now come sick people to be prayed for. Are you kidding me? If that were you, what would you do? What would you say to God and all the people watching? It is no sin to moan for the dead, especially if it was a family member. Even Jesus cried at the death of Lazarus. But Ma Phebe had to hold it in. Oh what a strong woman she is! I commend Ma Phebe.

Strangely, when Ma Phebe reached the sick people, she looked up to heaven and stretched her hands towards them, and said, "in the name of Jesus, rise up and walk," they all began to get up and were healed instantly! The cries and wailing were soon turned into a time of jubilation because of the healings. No one can truly describe this mixed feeling of mourning for a beloved son that now became overshadowed by miracles and healings. God sometimes does strange and magnificent things.

Now tell me, if you were Ma Phebe, what would you say to God and to the people? The same God who used you to heal many did not heal your beloved son. The week we buried Junior, one of our aunties from Zwedru, who came for the funeral, also died. The day they buried her, her sister who had lived with her in Zwedru, died too. Hence, in January Junior died, in February another death and in March, yet another death of a family member. But still, Ma Phebe continued praying and God was healing people.

Now you tell me, how can the same God of miracles who healed the sick through her not save Ma Phebe's family, allowing three to die in three months? Where was God? Why would he allow them to die, and yet use her to heal so many? Is her family not protected from an enemy or untimely death? And why would all of this happen to such a powerful woman of God? Why? Where was God when all of this happened to Ma Phebe?

# CHAPTER FIFTEEN

## A Bishop from Kenya

There is a heartbreaking story from Kenya that left my mouth open and caused deep heartbreak. This story raises the question of evil triumphing over good. It questions the level of security and assurance believers have in the Lord their God. It somewhat questions the character of God when it comes to his loving tender care for orphans and widows. It questions

God's protection for his servants, the carriers of the gospel of Christ Jesus, the pastors and ministers of God.

Not too long ago in Kenya, a well-known bishop in Nairobi, the capital of Kenya, a great man of God, was gunned down by unknown armed men. Here is the story from Worldwide Religious News in their article from July 4, 2010: [21] "Nairobi, Kenya - Gunmen shot dead a bishop in a midnight raid at a church in Nairobi's outskirts on Sunday.

Bishop Joseph Segel of the Redeemed Church, Ongata Rongai was shot twice in the chest as he attempted to block the attackers from entering the church. His wife Miriam hid at the altar while the gunmen beat up and frisked church faithful for valuables. Internal Security Minister George Saitoti visited the area on Wednesday last week and ordered the local police to beef up security, in response to yet another attack in which two people were hacked to death and 11 others injured a day earlier at Oloo Sirkon Village, seven kilometers away.

The church is located about 300 meters from the Ongata Rongai police station. The gunmen entered the church compound minutes after Miriam drove in, with the bishop on the passenger seat and three women were riding at the back. They were returning to the church late after attending a week-long 'religious mission' in Matuu. The three women are church faithful who had accompanied them for the mission. "It was some minutes to midnight. I took a turn from the tarmac road and was driving towards the church's gate. I saw a vehicle following from behind and I got nervous. I drove faster," Miriam said. She stopped at the gate and asked one of the ladies to alight and open the gate. 'I also told her to close and lock it immediately after I drove in,' added Miriam.

She parked the vehicle and entered the church through the office door while the ladies were unloading shopping bags when a gun appeared. "'I saw a very tall man with a rifle at the door. He was struggling with another man who is also a member of our church,' said Miriam. The other man is Mr. George Kamau, who said he'd been waiting to pray with the bishop, then spend the night at the church ahead of the morning service. 'It was 10 minutes to midnight. I helped open the gate and mama (Miriam) told me to monitor the other vehicle. It took a turn and drove past. But three men carrying firearms started to alight before the vehicle stopped and I dashed back,' he said.

He rushed back and alerted the ladies as they unloaded bags from the vehicle. "'I told them to rush and hide in the office. I followed them but as I entered the one with a rifle was right behind me. He kicked the door as it closed from inside. I fell on the floor and the bishop rushed to help. He shot him; then ordered us to lie on the floor, then shot him again,' added Mr. Kamau.

Two men had entered the church, the other had a pistol and another kept watch outside. "'They demanded the car keys and money. They also took a handbag and mobile phones and sped off,' Mr. Kamau said. A woman who had been left in the bishop's car was taken hostage as the gunmen sped off. The car, a Toyota Prado, was last morning found abandoned at the Kibera matatu termini and towed to Kilimani police station.

The woman was abandoned at Kenyatta market near the city's Ngumo estate. Miriam talked to her and she narrated her ordeal. 'In the car one of the gunmen broke down in tears and kept on saying. Mungu tusamehe Mungu tusamehe (Forgive us God). But another was rebuking him telling him there was no time for regrets,' the bishop's wife told the Nation. Elite detectives from Nairobi-based Flying squad and Special Crime Prevention Unit were dispatched to lead investigations into the matter. A somber mood engulfed the church service on Sunday. The sermon was disrupted at times, as faithful broke down in sobs and had to be helped out of the church. At the same time, detectives mingled with the faithful gathering clues on last night's incident.

At the bishop's home, a few kilometers away, other faithful, friends and relatives gathered to console the wife. The bishop had three children - Emmanuel, 16, Winner, 12 and three year-old Peace."

Wow, what a sad story! The bishop came from conducting a power-packed crusade where many lives were won to the Lord and great things happened. All the wonderful ministry did not keep arm robbers from abruptly ending his life in a very cruel way. How come, after God used him to bring salvation and encouragement to many, the same God who protects and does not let evil triumph over good, allowed this wonderful man of God to die in cold blood? He died in the compound of the church right before his wife and the others. Where was God? Why didn't he save the bishop and the others?

The bishop, returning from a weeklong crusade did not go straight home, but to the church to offer a prayer of thanksgiving, without any clue that he was just about to die. Was it wrong to give thanks to God first beyond going home to rest? This is so heartbreaking and difficult. It makes young Christians confused about the protection of God. It makes pastors of the gospel feel uneasy.

If a bishop, who just did some great ministry died in cold blood, then what about some of us? Many times it makes us to question our own humanity, and the potential of our own sudden violent demise. What is our assurance of protection for Christians? What is the assurance for protection for pastors? What is our fate as good people in the community? What becomes of the unbelievers when even the righteous seemed to have no security?

Are we now not safe and protected by the good God in heaven? Or we might say things like "God knows what is best; maybe that is how God planned his life," or 'it was just the devil's doing" – either way this questions the power and protection of God. It challenges the character of God. I don't know what the answer is; let me leave this one for all of us to ponder. But I must admit, these stories raise many questions. There are many other testimonies about God's miracle-working power in saving and rescuing people all across the globe. The question remains though, "where was God?" And really, where is God in all this?

# PART 5
# UNGRATEFUL HUMANITY

It is quite interesting that after many of us have prayed to God to help us with our problems we do not take time to thank him when we get our answers. This is a very terrible thing. We all have problem with ungrateful people. Such people, after we have helped them in their time of need, do not take time to thank us properly. It angers me. I think it will make anyone mad especially when I go out of our way to help people but then they never appreciate me for helping them.

Ungrateful people just love to get things from others but they do not give their gratitude for everything they now enjoy. This makes me unhappy and I believe many people feel the same way about ungrateful people. Now let us turn our minds up to heaven. Many times we ask God to help us with this and with that. We fast and pray; we do good works of service just for our answers to come. Some of us can even hire pastors, prophets, prayer people, friends and family to pray for us. We fast and pray and give anything to anyone to help us pray. After God answers our prayers, we forget everyone and forget about God.

All we do is to go about enjoying the blessings of God yet without a shred of gratitude to the one who gave the blessings. Many times we even forget the human elements God can use to help us in the process. Heaven looks at us in surprise and wonder what an ungrateful humanity

# CHAPTER SIXTEEN

## Heaven Asks Ungrateful Humanity

Finding God or asking "Where is God?" is a serious problem for both humanity and the kingdom of heaven. When something goes wrong, humanity boldly questions heaven, saying "Where is God?" because God has given the assurance that he will always be there and we know that we can count on him.

In spite of our position with God, we know the truth that whosoever shall call upon the name of the Lord shall be saved. So whether we are in good standing with God or not, we believe somehow that God will never fail us, even when we fail him, because he does not lie.

He loves us and can save us at any time when we are in trouble. Many of us take advantage of this by just wanting help from God but not God himself. That is why we have the tenacity and arrogance at times to ask "Where is God?" when trouble strikes.

It is also good to know that the angels and the entire kingdom of heaven also ask, "Where is God?" As ridiculous and surprising as it is, it is true. Interestingly, they do not ask themselves or ask heaven about God because God is in their midst and is the essence of their existence. Neither do they ask because they have a desire for answers and solutions like we do.

Unlike the purpose and quest of humanity to seek God's whereabouts, the angels and heaven ask us in disgust "Where is God?" for quite different reasons. They ask when we fail to acknowledge God for blessings that we enjoy. They ask why we, humanity, neglect to say "thank you" to God after our prayers are answered and we have solutions to our situations.

They ask because they see an ungrateful humanity that now enjoys prosperity, good health, good human relations, good jobs, prosperous businesses, happy marriages, growing churches, peaceful nations and God's favor, yet we have forgotten the giver - God.

They ask because they see humanity being too busy with God's good gifts and quickly forget that some of the gifts have expiration dates. They ask because they know that we will soon come back again to request more blessings. They wonder in despair about our reckless behavior of dashing God aside as we enjoy his benefits. They ask because they know that some of us will lose our place and position with God because of our behavior. They ask because we quickly forget to even thank the human agents of our blessings as we forget that it is God who makes those people to help us.

They ask because they know that some of us will never receive any such blessings from God again, as a testimony for others to see and learn how to say "thank you." Oh, the angels and the entire kingdom of heaven too is asking, "Where is God?" They are asking humanity, "Where is God?"

I can hear them asking every day. In fact, I can hear them asking you and I even right now, "Where is God?" The gospel writer Luke tells us a unique story about ungratefulness. Here is his account: [22] Now on his way to Jerusalem, Jesus traveled along the border between Samaria and Galilee. As he was going into a village, ten men who had leprosy met him. They stood at a distance and called out in a loud voice, "Jesus, Master, have pity on us!" When he saw them, he said, "Go, show yourselves to the priests." And as they went, they were cleansed.

When nine of them saw he was healed, came back, praising God in a loud voice. He threw himself at Jesus' feet and thanked him—he was a Samaritan. Jesus asked, "Were not all ten cleansed? Where are the other nine? Has no one returned to give praise to God except this foreigner?" Then he said to him, "Rise and go; your faith has made you well." Ungratefulness is a terrible sickness that brings anger, frustration and can cause us to miss out on future blessings.

When we thank someone for doing good to us, we say to them that we accept their kindness and we are glad they took time to think of us.

On the other hand, leaving without showing proper appreciation to those who helped us speaks against our integrity and negatively impacts the existing relationship. This is not good.

I wonder what will you and I say when the angels come asking why we are ungrateful. I do not know what it will be like when God takes away the blessings because we did not thank him properly, and the human proxies he used.

Exactly what will you say when they come to your home, your business, your church or place of entertainment; to your family, human relations and of course your marriage or relationship after you received from God the answers to your prayers. What will be your answer?

The next time you are ready to ask God for a blessing, please just look up and think where God will be in your life when he answers your prayers and works that issue out for you. You must also consider "Where is God?" after you who have received what you desire. Your response could affect your next request. Please learn to say thank you and be grateful.

Ungratefulness and forgetfulness is a sin on earth and in heaven. Do not become guilty as charged with ungratefulness. Start your day with a heart of thanksgiving and gratitude. Go find someone who treated you well and helped you, and thank them. They deserve it. Remember, it could be you who served, and I'll bet you would not appreciate such ingratitude. Be grateful. Say "thank you" to God and people. Some people are in the habit to only thank God and forget about the people he used to bring our blessings. Our ingratitude could prevent our next blessings. If you have people you have not thanked properly, please call or find them now and say "thank you". God is waiting. They are waiting; and of course, I am waiting. Be grateful.

# PART 6
# CONCLUSION: GOD IS THERE

I know it is disconcerting to say that God is there and he watches all the wickedness that happens in our world without stopping evil. When we think about rapists, child molesters, serial killers, gangsters, fraudsters, arm robbers, rebel leaders around the world and all the tyrannical leaders, it is hard to say that God is there watching without doing anything. But before we get all emotional and judgmental about God and his weakness over evil or carelessness towards suffering humanity, let me ask you this. When was the last time you did good things because they were good, even if it cost you something? When did you stop to defend justice and fight injustice to minorities and less privileged in your society?

What have you done about the suffering people in Africa, Indian, China, Latin America and other parts of the world and those in or around your area? What about the poor suffering kids on TV? I think you know where I am going with this. If we do not do our part of charity work to help the marginalized in our society, we do injustice. So how can unjust people like you and I who are guilty of greed, pride, and inhospitable character question the character and integrity of God by requesting him to do things we have been empowered to do? So before we start bashing God, let us examine ourselves first.

Yes, God is there; right there. He is wondering why we do not stop the evils in the world he has given us power to govern. God is wondering why a country like America that enjoys more than half of the goods of the world let the rest of the world suffer hunger, sickness and corruption.

God is wondering why Europe and America always rob poor undeveloped countries. God wonders why even in rich western countries there are hungry kids and homeless people. God wonders what is going on with us. God is always there. One day God will wipe away all our tears. This could be in heaven alas, or we could experience it right here on earth. God is there. As troubling as it may sound, the truth is He is right there in the worst of situations.

It is good to know that God is there for you in your good times and bad times. God truly is there. Please rest assure and know that things will be fine. I love a song that says, "anything that spoils, nobody can fi x it." No one can fi x it, only God can. Even if things are tough, God is there. He is there in good times; surely he is there in bad times. Remember, God is there regardless of how things are.

# CHAPTER SEVENTEEN

## It Could Be God

It is frightening to know that some of the "evils" that befalls us come from God. It is disconcerting to realize that some derogatory things come from God because the Bible teaches us that, [23] "every good gift and every perfect gift is from above, and comes down from the Father of lights, with whom there is no variation or shadow of turning."
It is also said of God that, [24] "he who did not spare his own son, but delivered him up for us all, how shall he not with him also freely give us all things?" This means that God gives good gifts indiscriminately to his people. So, if God is a loving father and a virtuous giver, how can evil come from God, or be accepted by God?
Undisputedly, it is true that God permits unfortunate things to happen to us, his children, his own creation. Why would God do this to us? Well, the answer sounds simple: It is a test. We may call it "evil," but to God, it is a necessary "evil" we might need to endure for our personal development. To God, it is not evil as a matter of fact. He sees it as a test, an opportunity for us to grow spiritually. God sees it as an open door we must walk through – a pathway to advancement

It is just a scrutiny to prepare us for the next level. There is a passage in the Bible that says, [25] "count it all joy when you fall into various trails, knowing that the testing of your faith produces patience. But let patience have its perfect work, that you may be perfect and complete, lacking nothing."

Sometimes I wonder to what degree we are to consider our troubles a test from God. How do we determine that? If they are tests, sometimes they surely seem like they were meant for our defeat because of the gravity. What puzzles me more than just knowing that God allows "evil" to happen to test us, is when God himself looks at an innocent man and gives permission to Satan to torture him.

According to a story I will tell, in spite of the man's dedication to God in prayers, and leading a righteous life, and benevolent, God still removed his protection from around the man and allowed Satan to destroy his family, his properties, his health, and in the end, almost destroyed him. Now, if it is true that God is a good and loving God, how can he orchestrate evil?"

I invite you to join me to visit the land of Uz and discuss one good man who did nothing wicked, yet God brought so much malevolence upon him. Bear with me as I bring you the story.

[26] In the land of Uz there lived a man whose name was Job. He was blameless and upright; he feared God and shunned evil. He had seven sons and three daughters, and he owned seven thousand sheep, three thousand camels, five hundred yoke of oxen and five hundred donkeys, and had a large number of servants. He was the greatest man among all the people of the East.

His sons used to hold feasts in their homes on their birthdays, and they would invite their three sisters to eat and drink with them. When a period of feasting had run its course, Job would make arrangements for them to be purified. Early in the morning he would sacrifice a burnt offering for each of them, thinking, "Perhaps my children have sinned and cursed God in their hearts." This was Job's regular custom. One day the angels came to present themselves before the LORD, and Satan also came with them. The LORD said to Satan, "Where have you come from?"

Satan answered the LORD, "From roaming throughout the earth, going back and forth on it." Then the LORD said to Satan, "Have you considered my servant Job? There is no one on earth like him; he is blameless and upright, a man who fears God and shuns evil." "Does Job fear God for nothing?" Satan replied. "Have you not put a hedge around him and his household and everything he has? You have blessed the work of his hands, so that his flocks and herds are spread throughout the land. But now stretch out your hand and strike everything he has, and he will surely curse you to your face."

The LORD said to Satan, "Very well, then, everything he has is in your power, but on the man himself do not lay a finger." Then Satan went out from the presence of the LORD." So is the Bible saying that God commissioned Satan to rain havoc on Job's life? Let us summarize the story. Job had ten children; seven sons and three daughters. One day Job would experience his worst day for which he would demand God's justice and wonder why God allows bad things to happen to good people. Let's get started in the order of the events that almost ended Job's life.

1. The Sabean raiders took all of Job's oxen and donkeys and killed the servants, except one. Only one managed to escape and brought the news.
2. The fire of God fell from heaven and burned all of the sheep and other servants; he too barely escaped.
3. The Chadeans formed three bands, raided the camels and killed more servants; one was lucky to run.
4. A storm arose, destroying the house of the eldest son, and all of Job's ten children died while they were having a party. One servant barely managed to escape to report the tragedy.

All of these terrible things happened in one day! Just one lucky servant would escape death to run and tell Job as the other ended his part of the story. All of this happened, one after-the-other. I wonder if this were you or I, what would happen to us? Would we faint, have a stroke, would our blood pressure go up or sugar level rise too high? Or what would actually happen to you? Would you die? I hope not. As Job and his wife were gathering their lives after the loss of their children, servants, animals and properties, yet another round of evil befell him, adding insult to injury. Life was miserable for him.[27] On another day, the angels came to present themselves before the LORD, and Satan also came with them to present himself. The LORD said to Satan, "Where have you come from?" Satan answered the LORD, "From roaming throughout the earth, going back and forth on it." Then the LORD said to Satan, "Have you considered my servant Job? There is no one on earth like him; he is blameless and upright, a man who fears God and shuns evil. And he still maintains his integrity, though you incited me against him to ruin him without any reason." "Skin for skin!" Satan replied. "A man will give all he has for his own life. But now stretch out your hand and strike his flesh and bones, and he will surely curse you to your face."

The LORD said to Satan, "Very well, then, he is in your hands; but you must spare his life." So Satan went out from the presence of the LORD and afflicted Job with painful sores from the soles of his feet to the crown of his head. Then Job took a piece of broken pottery and scraped himself with it as he sat among the ashes.

His wife said to him, "Are you still maintaining your integrity? Curse God and die!" He replied, "You are talking like a foolish woman. Shall we accept good from God, and not trouble?" Why did God and the devil keep disturbing Job's life? Does God take pleasure in the suffering of his children, or what sort of game is this? Look at the third paragraph above, the devil demands "skin for skin" and God surprisingly says yes. It is difficult to say that God is a good God especially, when he allows things like this.

Another round of terrible things happened to Job. When he lost his body to sickness with nasty sores that itched and took over his body, his wife turned on him and his trust in God because things were so terrible. Of all people, his wife was ready to walk out on him. Isn't it rather interesting to know that at the time we need friends and family most, is when they usually get tired with our situation and walk away? It can be so difficult when trusted friends and family do this. It can be so hurtful.

Job had three friends who taunted him daily and accused him for sinning against God when Job had done absolutely nothing wrong. Well, we must thank God for people like Job who stood the test of time and kept the faith. At the end of this story, God finally broke his silence, rebuked Job's friends, and dealt with Job and restoring to him double than his former days. For God, what we call "evil", "bad things" or "bad luck" is only like a test that schools offer to students to evaluate for promotion. Sadly, to some of the students the test, which is an opportunity to prove oneself as having proper knowledge of the material, it is evil because they are not well prepared.

Some students feel the teachers or the school may be trying to fail them or retain them in the same class. Students complained against the teachers and the school. It seemed to them that some conspiracy was transpiring, when the truth is that they were presented with an opportunity for promotion. Yet to the students who work hard to study and prepare for the test, it is just a matter of promotion. It is a good opportunity to prove what they are capable of. That is what God expects of us. So before you ask, "Where is God?" when life comes at you, please ask yourself whether this is a test. Is this a test that you are expected to pass with honors for your next promotion, or how do you see it?

# CHAPTER EIGHTEEN

## Personal Failures

The Bible declares that [28] all have sinned and fallen short of the glory of God", and that [29] the wages of sin is death, but the gift of God is eternal life in Christ Jesus our Lord." This addresses three things: all have sinned, wages of sin is death, and God has given a gift of eternal life in Jesus. The issue of personal failures is very sensitive and critical. We must apply all caution as we endeavor to discuss with others their failures; otherwise we will fall into the abyss of creating more damage to those people than actually helping them.

Many people from whom we seek advice sometimes tell us that the truth can hurt and so we must embrace the truth, and make all necessary adjustments if we are to move forward in life. Well spoken, but the problem I have with people who boldly speak the truth to us in our situations is the manner in which such truths are presented.

Many of the good people who advise us in our times of failure are insensitive to our feelings. The way they might say things can become insulting. Rather, they should carefully tell us the reality of our condition and show us a way out. When we feel insulted and shamed, we have two options: to fight back or accept and adjust, depending on the situation. Many of us remain in our failures even after counseling, or just simple advice from family or friends, because of the way they addressed us.

When the truth of our situation is told in a way that insults and condemns us, our natural response becomes to fight back. When this happens, we might not want to deal with the issue anymore. Many times, we have hopelessly failed the hurting in their situation. There are three people found in the Bible we will discuss about their failures and their responses, and see how we can learn from that. The people were leaders; as a matter of fact, God chose them. They were capable of leadership and had great responsibility.

### King Saul of Israel:

Saul was called by God and anointed by the prophet Samuel to become the first king of Israel. Saul was the right size and height for a king. He did not lobby for kingship, but God chose him as the answer to Israel's prayer for a king. Saul enjoyed the favor and protection of God for years. He ruled Israel and won battles. There was a good working relationship between King Saul and the Prophet Samuel for years. Samuel declared victory over any enemy of Israel, Saul obtained the victory according to the word of God, through Samuel.

It was a wonderful thing, until one battle when Saul ran out of patience and did things Samuel told him not to do and did things Samuel never told him never to do. Because of this offense, the word of God came through Samuel as usual, except this time it was to reject Saul as King over Israel. Saul tried to beg immediately, but there were even more issues at stake: the existence of the nation Israel and its future were bleak because of his actions. Instead of carefully pleading, he held onto the garment of Samuel until he tore it off. Samuel proclaimed more damage unto Saul and his kingship, and he was rejected.

Sometime later, Prophet Samuel anointed David as the new

king over Israel when Saul was still king. This angered King Saul. Instead of seeking God's face to receive forgiveness and secure his throne, Saul sought to kill David to protect his kingship – the kingship he knew nothing about and given to him by God without any labor. To make things worse, Prophet Samuel died without granting King Saul any forgiveness according to the word of the Lord.

When the enemies gathered against Israel, King Saul remembered his old working relations with Samuel. So Saul went to inquire of Samuel whether God would grant him victory as before, except this time Samuel was dead. Saul went to a witch who was a medium, to invoke Prophet Samuel's spirit to speak to him.

What a terrible mistake! In Prophet Samuel's lifetime and during his ministry he had killed witches because they polluted the people with divination and idolatry. Sadly, Saul went to a female witch, a sorcerer, to bring back Samuel's spirit to speak to him about the war at hand. The truth is that Prophet Samuel's spirit arose and spoke to King Saul, but what happened was nothing Saul expected.

Instead of declaring victory to Saul and defeat to the enemy, Samuel rebuked Saul that he used a medium instead of asking God's help, and because of that, his declaration was that Israel would lose the battle, King Saul and his three sons would die in battle. Samuel's spirit departed and Saul left in disgust, forced to go to war knowing that he would die with his sons, and Israel would be badly defeated. Oh Saul, why did you disturb Samuel?

Look at the loss King Saul and Israel had to suffer. Be it known unto you and please tell others that it is a very bad thing to anger the man or woman who represents God. The results are catastrophic!

Do not end up like King Saul of Israel. In talking about personal failures, a favored Saul who became the first king of Israel became disfavored because he failed to follow simple instructions. Instead of finding better ways to resolve the issue, he continually plunged himself into more trouble that led to his death and terrible loss to Israel. I hope as you read about Saul, you will take appropriate steps to deal with your failures.

## Sampson - A Judge in Israel:

Sampson was born to become the leader of Israel in a time when there was neither king nor prophet, but only judges to govern the people. He was born a Nazarene; meaning he was not to drink any alcohol, nor cut or shave his hair. His power was in his hair. The spirit of the Lord was upon him for the sole purpose of protecting Israel against the advance of the Philistines.

When Sampson came of age, a wife was arranged for him, as was customary. Sadly, Sampson refused the chosen woman. His parents and the council urged him to look throughout Israel and find the wife of his choice. Unfortunately, Sampson did not have any interest in Israelite women because the only woman he loved was from Philistia – a woman from the enemy's camp.

It is very important for us to listen to the good advice of our parents and guidance in choosing a wife or husband. Some things are simple to explain when it comes to relationships; but sometimes our family just have a way to know the bad future that awaits if we go on marrying the person against their advice. They may not have any better way to explain their feelings, but it is good to listen. Beware folks.

Regardless of the advice from his family and leaders, Sampson pursued Delilah, a Philistine woman – of the same people he fought constantly. When the leaders of Philistia became aware that their worst enemy, Sampson, was sleeping with Delilah's, they made a deal with Delilah and her family to kill him.

They engineered Delilah to ask Sampson about the source and secret of his strength. Delilah and her family accepted the deal and soon began to lure Sampson into telling her the secret of his strength so as to kill him. Sampson lied to her during her first few attempts on his life, and he destroyed the enemies. Instead of Sampson realizing that Delilah was up to something, and that something was to have him killed, he was seeing it as a game. He thought that he would always win.

I assume Sampson did read some of the accounts of Abraham who endangered his family life by using his wife Sarah as bait to gain wealth. Even though Abraham was a friend of God and the father of the nation Israel and of our Christian faith, at times he did not trust God for provisions. He used his faith only to trust God to protect Sarah and get the provisions from the rich. Abraham did this "4-1-9" thing couple of times and God interestingly protected him and his wife, Sarah. God was his wingman.

I bring up Abraham because if Sampson knew the story as I would think, perhaps he might have thought to himself, if Abraham used Sarah to obtain riches, he could use Delilah to kill more Philistines, even in the bedroom at her father's house in the Philistine camp! Such arrogance and misuse of God's name and power did not fend well for Sampson in the end.

There is a wise saying in Liberia that says, [30] "goat's luck and sheep's luck is not the same." This simply means that no two persons are the same, even if they are twins; so do not do anything just because another person did it and got away with it or had a fortune in it. I wish I was there to tell Sampson he should only use Abraham as his role model in a positive way and not like that.

Against reason and family advice, Sampson did not help himself but continue to love Delilah, instead of finding a beautiful virgin Jewish girl for a wife. This rebellion, after all of God's previous protection, grace and opportunities to repent, led Sampson to meet his fate – an untimely death.

Delilah wearied Sampson to the point that he "spilled the beans" by telling her that the real source of his strength was his hair. What was meant for his power and protection later became his vulnerability – the very reason for his demise. I tell you, some things of importance are better kept private. Please don't just open your mouth to people and talk certain things.

After being drunk with much wine and lust, perhaps Sampson was enjoying a soft massage and tender caressing of his body with wounds from the day's battle. Maybe he laid his head on Delilah soft thighs with her breasts pressing gently toward his face, and began to talk. Sampson talked until he revealed the key to his strength and the best way to kill him.

## WHERE IS GOD?

Sometimes it is best not to talk too much. Some of us get into trouble, not because of the devil or other people; it is simply because we do not control our mouths. We can keep talking until it gets us in trouble. When Sampson told Delilah that cutting his hair would cause him to lose his strength, she put it to the test right away. Sampson's enemies, her people, came in immediately, and shaved his hair and tied him. To make things worse for Sampson, they plugged out his eyes so he would never see daylight again. Sampson never saw Delilah or anything again. To make a long story short, Sampson could not fight back as usual – he could not rise up and kill the Philistines.

Unlike Abraham, who always got away with "4-1-9", Sampson was not so lucky. God did not show up for him on just this one occasion and he lost everything. When he lost the strength to fight back because he had broken the Nazarene vow and allowed his hair to be cut, his enemies seized the opportunity and struck him down. They bound him with great chains and gouged out his eyes so he would never see again. The great giant and warrior of Israel, who had won battles against the Philistines, became a blind show boy for Philistine entertainment. Oh, Sampson, why? How could you join the strong men that women have brought down? I hope you and I will not be like other mighty men and women who were destroyed by sex and corrupt company. Beware, not everything that glitters is diamond; even broken glass glitters too!

While this was a sad thing for Sampson and Israel, the Philistines rejoiced greatly at the capture of the once-dreaded man that broke through their defense and constantly reduced their population. The mighty warrior of Israel now became the topic of the day as a "beast captured by a little princess."

Delilah and her family gained wealth and popularity to the loss of Sampson and Israel.

During the festivals, they would bring out Sampson to amuse them. Having removed his eyes, they would mock him and play war games with Sampson, knowing that he lost his strength and his sight. They taunted him and mocked him in their songs.

There is one festival Philistia would never forget, a celebration to their god, Dagon, for giving them victory over Sampson and Israel. They enjoyed feasting as usual, but they forgot that Sampson's hair had begun to grow back. Knowing that his hair represented his strength, they forgot as they began to be merry. Sampson started to regain strength, but he kept it as a secret and eagerly awaited the next festival to strike back.

After patiently waiting for some time, during that time there was a huge cerebration with all the leaders of the nation, princes, generals of the army, choirs, performers and beautiful ladies. Delilah and her family were in the best seats, and with much wine to drink, they had Sampson on waiting to perform as usual. But unlike the past, Sampson did not wait for their signal. He asked a servant boy to position him between the two main pillars that held the building together.

The servant boy positioned Sampson correctly; and Sampson told him to depart at once. Sampson gathered himself and prayed one desperate prayer that I love very much. It was a dangerous prayer uttered out of deep desperation. It was a prayer to pray perhaps just once in our lifetime, to get catastrophic effects. It was a prayer to silence an unbearable condition once and for all. It was truly the type of prayer that you pray when you are at the end of the tunnel and have no way out. It was such a prayer that Moses expressed before the Red Sea when he and the children of Israel had no way out. With Pharaoh and his chariots blocking their way, rocky cliffs on both sides and a vast sea ahead of them, it had to be God who would make divine intervention. In dire predicaments, it takes desperate prayers for these situations.

For Moses and Israel, God divided the Red Sea like a wall and made dry land in the middle for Israel to pass through. The chariots of Pharaoh wanted to grace the same path Israel took; but things did not go well for them. Prayers were not made for them; so the sea refused them passage and swallowed them up.

Let's get back to Sampson for a minute. I just wanted to show you the power of desperate prayers and how God can be faithful, even after we have sinned and blundered. On that day of their festivity, Sampson cried out to God in desperation, saying "Oh, Lord God, remember me, I pray! Strengthen me, I pray, just this once. Oh, God, that I may with a blow take vengeance on the Philistines for my two eyes!" Let me digress and ask you one question. What have you lost to an enemy? What have you lost because of your mistakes, or because people hate you, or because of doing what is right?

I urge you to pray a desperate prayer like Sampson did when you have had enough and can take it no more. Say to the people or thing that enough is enough, and cry out to God sincerely. As he heard Sampson, he will hear you and intervene. If you do not mind, I suggest that you pause now and say a little prayer. I strongly believe that God will work it out for you. Let our spirits connect with the Creator right now. I feel that someone needs to pray right now. If that is you, I commit myself to you in prayer. I declare that it shall be well with you in the mighty name of Jesus. I command that situation to go now. Amen.

If you prayed that little but powerful prayer, thank you. I believe God will visit you. If you do not believe in prayer or in God, I hope you will one day. I remember praying a similar prayer some time ago when I was caught in a situation where I was pressed against the wall.

I did not know what to do or who to call. Everyone got tired of me. Some people just waited to see my demise so I could make their day in gossip.

But when I desperately and purposely applied the God factor in my calamity, I received my breakthrough. If you have prayed that kind of prayer from your heart, I implore that God will visit you and give your own testimony, even as he did for me. Sampson ended his prayer of desperation by saying, "Let me die with the Philistines," and he died. One interesting point in Sampson's situation was that the slaughter he had in his last and desperate move was even greater than all the ones he had in real battles.

Sampson pray to die with the enemy; I do not pray that prayer. I pray to overcome my weakness and overcome the enemy. I do not want to die with the enemy in battle. I want to live to tell the story. I want to tell the goodness of the Lord in the land of the living. I want others to know that the same God who helped me out can help them too.

I believe God did not just answer Sampson's prayer, but he stood for Israel that had just lost a mighty warrior, by killing more people and destroying all the manpower that would mount further attacks. In the case of Sampson, his weakness and failure was woman, a strange but beautiful woman named Delilah. Sampson died in regret, except that he rejoiced when God gave him strength for the last time to deal the enemy a terrible blow.

Had Sampson listened to his father and the elders to take a different wife, a Jewish girl, I believe God would have given them victory over Philistia without such tragedy. Let's learn from Sampson, because we may not be as lucky as Abraham.

### King David of Israel:

David was a king of Israel with many wives. At times I have wondered how the king became intimate with these hundreds of wives. If he took them two a day, how many months would pass before he could see the same woman again? Wow, King David was really the ladies' man! Yet, with all that, the king who should have been in battle leading his troops decided to stay home and do nothing.

As we discussed before, it was at such a time with an idle mind, while walking on his balcony that he saw a married woman named Bathsheba bathing. I believe the king saw the naked woman by mistake, but instead of catching himself and focusing elsewhere, he began to look at her deeply and admired her beauty. King David immediately sent for Bathsheba and soon after, a secret love affair began, and Bathsheba became pregnant with his child. Adultery was a sin with harsh punishment – death – and the king knew it. Yet he had sex with this woman and made her pregnant. To cover the sin of adultery, King David sent for her husband, tried to get him drunk and sent him home to sleep with his wife.

## WHERE IS GOD?

The good soldier refused to sleep in the comfort of his wife, knowing how terrible the battle was. And remembering his friends in the line of fire, he did not comply with the king's plan for cover-up. When that failed, David had the innocent soldier killed in battle and then took his wife as his own, adding one more to his multiple transgressions. A short time later, a man of God, Nathan, approached David and changed the story in which David accused and condemned himself for his act of adultery. Nathan pronounced death unto the baby he and Bathsheba had. The baby died according to the word of God.

Unlike King Saul who never repented, but provoked a dead prophet that caused his own death and that of his sons, and cause loss to Israel, David repented. Unlike Sampson, who did not listen to advice from his parents and the elders of Israel, but prayed a desperate prayer to die with the enemy, David admitted his sins right away, repented and asked for God to forgive him.

Fortunately, God answered David's prayer and forgave him. The adultery and murder were forgiven and David kept Bathsheba as his wife. They later had a son named Solomon, who became the next king of Israel. Even though the penalty for David's sins had more consequences than what I told you, with all that mess he caused himself, his family and the nation Israel, God forgave him. God forgave him of the adultery and of the murder and redeemed him from all the other terrible consequences of his actions. David remained king until he appointed Solomon as the new king, and after some time he died in peace.

We have all sinned and fallen short of the glory of God. Oh yes, there is none totally righteous, not one. And yes, when we say we have no sin, we lie and the truth is not found because we have a sinful nature. But in spite of that, the grace of God has given us power over sin and evil so that once we give our lives to God, his righteousness comes upon us and our sinful nature dies.

We can choose to sin or not, and if we want to remain faithful to God, there is enough grace to help us even though we are not perfect. So we do not really have to dwell in sin or magnify our weakness, because God has given us power to overcome. I say that you and I have a choice to make when we sin. You can be arrogant like King Saul and die in pity without repentance. You can also be like Sampson who repented too late but died with the enemy. Perhaps you can be like King David, who after committing gross sin, prayed to God for forgiveness and repented. God completely forgave him and restored him. David kept his position until he died.

We all make mistakes; and our mistakes can sometimes cost us too much. Regardless of the price of your weakness and the damage rendered, there is still room at the cross for people like you and me. Do not be like Saul, who never repented out of arrogance and tried to raise the dead Prophet Samuel to give him answers. Please do not be like Sampson, who against all good advice gave himself so cheaply to the enemy. In pains, agony and misery, he lived in mockery until the day he repented and asked God for just one wish; he prayed the desperate prayer and died.

Though God answered Sampson, he did not live to see what God did for him and Israel. Sampson died with the enemy. I pray that it will not be too late for you when your answer comes. May God answer your prayers for you to live to tell the story. I do not want to hear about your big victories during your funeral. You can live to tell your own story about the goodness of God as it was in the case of David.

Our weaknesses can break us or make us. It is up to the way we play our cards or let others do it for us. Whatever life brings, in your time of weakness, mistakes and shameful acts,

I urge you to remember King David. God's grace is sufficient. David was the "man after God's own heart" when he was a shepherd boy and anointed to be the king of Israel, even though at that time, he was a "nobody." He was still that same man when he sinned grossly against God and others – the time when he was "somebody" and interestingly because of his heart, he remained the "man after God's own heart" until he died. You can get yourself out of the mess and live to tell the story. Go on!

I have failures and you have failures. Hey, who else are you thinking about, they have failures as well. The people that look perfect to you also have failures. Your pastor, yes I mean your pastor, has failures. That sweet, hot and sexy girl has failures. And, true enough, that hot guy with the sexy abs has failures.

Everyone has failures and weaknesses. The important matter is not our failure, but rather how we gather ourselves to move on. When we literally fall while walking we do not remain on the ground unless we sprang or break something; we usually get up and continue. So, let us move on.

The Apostle Paul said something I love in his letter to the Philippians. He said, [31] forgetting those things which are behind and reaching forward to those things which are ahead." Let me tell you something. I have things I put behind me that you do not want to know about; I have learned to leave the past in the past.

While it is true that we should sometimes remember our past, it should not be to the extent it holds hostage our present and robs us of our future. The truth is that in our past are some victories and happy times we love to talk about. It is also true that many of us also have some terrible, embarrassing, shameful and demeaning stories that we do not want anybody to know about. If you are a saint, I thank God for you; but some of us have some little stories.

These failures or weaknesses brought us pain, regret, shame and agony. Some of them were very humiliating and that is why I join Paul to say forget the past and press toward the future. You can still make it regardless of your failures and weaknesses. People may reject you in some places; it is okay, move on. You are wanted in other places; go on.

People may label you as "good for nothing," a "looser" or "drop-out," but God will always say you are good for something. To be frank, you are the best for the job. God has something special in store for you; please work with God to discover it.

Therefore, do not let your failures or weaknesses hold you from charting the course of the life that God has given you. Grab your destiny, live it and enjoy it. We all have just one life to live here on earth. Why make it any more miserable than it has to be. Come on, dear, put yourself together. Subdue your flaws and play them to your strength, and you will see how insignificant they will be over time. Let us say together, "God is there; right there. With God, I can do all things!"

# CHAPTER NINTEEN

# The Devil

In our world today, many modern people across the globe do not believe in the supernatural – be it heaven or hell, God or Satan. They simply employ reason and rationalize everything. Whatever cannot be proven by science or connect with the senses they dismiss as frivolous. As far as they are concerned, only poor people need God or mystical things. Only the weak need religion and not learned or affluent people. God or the supernatural has no room in their lives.

When I was much younger, we use to say a proverb that says "sticks and stones hurt my bones, but words cannot hurt me." Wow, that sounds convincing, except that it is not true. I wish it was true as it sounds. I think by now, you and I should know that things can hurt us beyond sticks and stones. As a matter of fact, many of us have never been hurt by sticks or stones, but we carry so many scars in our lives.

We experience a lot of things physically, emotionally, psychologically and mentally. But I want to tell you that some things are spiritual – they are supernatural. There is a fight we should be aware of. It is a fight between good and evil. By using the word evil, we talk about the principal "evil" – the devil or Satan and his cohorts. When we talk about good we refer to God, Jesus and the kingdom of God.

By now, you and I should know that when there is a spiritual problem, the manifestation is usually physical, emotional and psychological. While it is true that we don't always see evil spirits, powers and principalities, the effects of such evils are prevalent in our world today.

For some modern-day blessed people, spiritual matters are seen as what the poor and needy require since they are unfortunate enough not to have gained wealth. They think it is the poor and needy that look around for the saviors that rich people do not need. They think their money and science can do everything.

Unfortunately, the truth is that the devil can haunt the wealthy and the poor alike. As a matter of fact, he likes the rich because he knows that they use their wealth to do much harm to others, both in undeveloped and developed countries. I believe Satan loves the prosperous people more because he can use them as a tool to heap plenty suffering upon the poor and corrupt modern societies. The wealthy can exploit the poor and provide them with guns and cash to make them fight and kill one another. They create wars, starvation, rape, murder and destroy infrastructure and kill the future of people.

The wicked rich in the hands of the devil can cause unimaginable dangers. Just look around Africa and Latin America to see what I am talking about. The affluent, the strong and mighty in the hands of the devil can cause much harm – reflect on Adolf Hitler and the Holocaust. One man killed five million Jews and caused world wars. Just think about the great loss of lives and properties and the hatred that remained thereafter.

I am not yet talking about the issue of witchcraft, sorcery, voodoo and vampires; we will get to that. But the mass murders and atrocities committed by the mighty against the innocent poor is so appalling. Think about World Wars I and II. Think about what detrimental weaponry like atomic bombs accomplished. Consider Pearl Harbor and Hiroshima, and the aftermath.

It is also true that the devil can use the affluent to destroy people in developed countries through the internet, drugs, pornography, gangs, guns, terrorism, computer scams, crashing stock markets, gambling, and more. The internet has become a place of mass sin and evil. Social networks of today, as good as they are to help us connect with others, can be used to destroy lives so easily.

With television, computers and fast internet on mobile phones, with apps that do virtually anything desirable, and with porn as one of the hottest apps, many teenagers watch porn on their phones. No wonder our boys and girls have become so sexually active. Parents, schools and religious institutions do not have to worry about the wearisome subject of sex education, because TV, computers and mobile phones have already taught our beautiful kids about sex in detail, way beyond our comfort levels.

If you were to ask an adolescent boy or girl in the developed world about what sex is, many of them will respond, "What type of sex?" meaning, the category of sex you want to talk about. Such answer would tell a parent that the child is well-informed about sex. As a matter of fact, it can tell you a gist of their experience and involvement with sex.

This might sound strange to parents from strict religious upbringing, but the truth is that even most of our kids have watched porn on their phones and computers, or on cable TV.

Whether you believe in the existence of evil or not, the truth is that evil affects all of us, and some of the things we deal with have their origins in spiritual things – it is only the physical exhibition we experience.

There are certain things people can do that are ridiculous, and the best way to describe their actions is to use the word, "devilish" – it can only be attributed to the character of the devil. All over America and Europe and many other places are people known as serial killers. They know the art of killing people and terrorizing communities for the pleasure of it.

They subject their victims to rape, torture and prolonged sufferings before they discard them. They kill innocent people and keep their bodies or dispose them for the public to see. News and sights of such deaths can inflict fear into large communities. The evil perpetrators might see it as their trophies or rewards – it is like the community is praising them for their art work.

Now let us turn our minds to the issue of witchcraft in Africa, India and other parts of the world. Whether you believe in the existence and power of witchcraft or not, the power of witchcraft is real and can hurt people. On a higher level, anyone can be a victim of witches, except for those who are born again and protected by God. The devil can assign agents to you and me to reduce us to nothing or make us carriers of evil without our consent. There are some people who are involved in witchcraft by choice, some are born into it and some are given to pregnant women as babies to fulfill a certain destiny in raining down evil on God's people.

There are groups and categories of witches and wizards. There are levels of powers, territories and evil requirements involved for their maintenance and procedures. Some are marine spirits; others dwell in the upper spheres, while others live in deserted places and cemeteries. There are some higher demons and evil spirits that dwell among us and masquerade as humans.

They are truly not human, but evil spirits living as physical beings that resemble people.

In female forms they can be attractive and whoever sleeps with them is initiated into witchcraft or becomes a victim. In male forms they are wealthy men maturing in secret societies and involved in the occult. People are carried away by their wealth and charity they do becomes a problem for the receiver.

Whether people become wicked, evil, witches killing and destroying, or centers for initiation in secret societies, into dangerous occults that demand human blood, human parts and human sacrifice, or create conditions to increase human suffering, one thing we can believe is that witchcraft and the devil together with his cohorts are alive and dangerous. Regardless of how terrible, fearful or beautiful they appear, where they dwell, or what powers they possess, they are no match for the power of God. As a matter of fact, they are afraid of the name of Jesus. But I caution you not to use the name of Jesus recklessly because it has power.

The devil is smart enough to know whether you and I have rights and privileges to the name of Jesus based on our relationship with God. It would be a dangerous thing to use the name of Jesus to cast out devils and demons if we do not have Jesus in our lives. The devil can read through us and attack us, and surely enough, we could be hurt. The best thing to do is to acknowledge our weaknesses, confess our sins, and ask for forgiveness. We must ask Jesus to come into our lives to be our Lord and savior. With Jesus in our lives as our personal savior and Lord, we can legitimately use his name to fight the devil.

Otherwise, it is a very risky maneuver. It is true that you do not have to believe it to be affected. As a matter of fact, the naïve can become a very easy target and the next innocent victim. There are people I know in whose family no one graduates from high school. Another family had women that never married or no one can do good business. In others, people die early and in strange ways. I also know of a family in which the men can never succeed. It is like every bad thing in life was intended for them. There are myriads of stories I know of that defile logic; but the only way out is to say it is evil and cling to the Lord.

Some of these people were delivered through fervent prayers; but there are some families that still suffer the problems today because of their disbelief in God. The devil knows very well how to inflict evil and hardship on people and make them hopeless, so that they never seek help. If you run into the people I am talking about, you should share your sympathy because their conditions are so deplorable.

The devil has three objectives: to steal, kill, and destroy. He can make things go bad for you and steal your bright future. He can make you miss good opportunities and things that you know you qualify for and deserve. He can make people who said "yes" to you change their minds and later, and do not even want to hear your name, much less see you. The devil is stealing the life of our men and women. He is stealing the future of our boys and girls.

The devil can steal the future of a whole group or community and keep them in bondage. The devil specializes in theft. He steals and lies very well. The devil can kill you if you are not in

## WHERE IS GOD?

God. He can kill you at his whim at any time; but he'd rather torture you or make you his agent. In this way, you are more useful to the kingdom of the devil than just slaying your body and soul for entertainment.

The destruction of the devil is excruciating and very ruthless. The devil may not wish to kill you, but he can destroy your life in sickness, terrible accidents, other troubles, and cause huge loss in marriage, family, business, church, education, work, and render you useless to society. The devil knows how to destroy people. Words are limited to describe how devastating the actions of the devil can be in destroying people. He does not just destroy one person, he destroys families and generations, and can block success on every side to make them suffer.

In the midst of their troubles, people can live in tears and wonder, asking "Where is God?" The devil can create conditions to make people doubt even the very existence of God. For Christians and other good people, it appears that the day they gave their lives to God, that is the day their troubles began.

It has made some think the devil has more power than God, because what they see around them is the infliction of the devil and not the deliverance of God. The devil can make people live in depression rather than put smiles on their faces. Every day feels gloomy and nothing works out but darkness and premonitions come. The devil can make the night fearful and the days very long for those who do not have God as their defender.

While I do not want to take so much time magnifying the devil, because I am not here to praise him, I want to stress the point that the devil exists and is desperately wicked. Whether you believe it or not, the devil can rain havoc upon humanity. One woman in my church got a call from her uncle in Monrovia, Liberia asking for more money for his business and her ear became deaf just two days after they argued about $250.00 she sent him.

The uncle expected $500.00 so the $250.00 she sent did not please him and a bitter argument arose. He called her two days later and asked, "is this Jane Doe?" She answered yes, and he hung up. Her daughters wanted to talk to their uncle, and while talking with them about it, she noticed her ear that she used during his call had gone deaf. You may call it coincidence, but I call it witchcraft. We took her to the church and prayed for her. Thank God she received her hearing back her immediately.

One New Year's Day, I went to the church early in the morning to pray. As soon as I put the key in the door, I felt something come upon me and the hair on my body stood up. I entered the church, prayed for an hour and left. After I got in the car and while trying to reverse, I looked into the rearview mirror and saw that my left eye was blood-red. It did not itch or hurt at the time and nothing had gotten into my eye, so I could not understand why it became red.

Just two minutes after I drove off into the traffic, I felt a sharp pain in my eye. It was so severe that I could feel it in the back of my head and in my ear. I hurried home, but it was as if my world was coming to an abrupt end. My eyes began to run, my head hurt and I started to shed tears from the extreme pain. I meant to greet one of my deacons, but as soon as I got home, I rushed past him and went straight into the bedroom and called out to my wife.

When she saw my eye and how I was hurting she began to cry and called for an ambulance. I motioned her to put the phone down and I told her we needed to pray. We prayed for a while and the pains subsided, I came out to explain to my deacon about what was happening. As I was talking to him about my eye, he looked at it and seeing how bad it was, he shared his sympathy with me.

While we were talking, his wife's phone rang as she entered the house. The wife of one of the break-away pastors called her to tell her this: "I just called to tell you that they played witch on Pastor James at the church; but he did not die." The deacon's wife screamed and asked where she got such things from, and the lady hung up the phone. That call left all of us in bewilderment, and it confirmed my position that it was the devil's doing.

The deacon asked me right away whether this lady or anyone else was at the church when I was there. I told him no, I was alone that early morning. Then the deacon began to ask how this lady who was not at the church knew that I was at the church, and that I was bewitched. How? Who told her? We were all perplexed, but I knew it was the devil behind the attack.

The next day I visited my doctor who sent me to an eye, nose and ear specialist and they ran multiple tests on me. He concluded that I had some terrible complication which required surgery. He assured me that I would be okay and able see normally in one week after the procedure. Still in pain, I gathered myself and told the doctor that I was a pastor and so I would not do the surgery. As a matter of fact, I told him I was not going to see him again because I did not need the surgery. I did not want the surgery because I was going to the church to pray. I believed I would be just fine once I prayed again.

That American doctor did not understand what I meant and he told me that he has been treating a lot of pastors and assured me that he would take care of me too. I disappointed him I when told him to excuse me because I was on my way to the church to pray. I reached out my hand and thanked him for his time but said I was going to apply faith. I left him in surprise.

I asked myself the same question: "Where is God?" Moreover, I made it personal and I said, "Where is my God before this American doctor wants to open my head to do surgery on my eyes, nose and ears?" As good as he was, I couldn't let him do the procedure because I knew my God would heal me.

To be frank, as stupid as I am, what would become of me when they split open my head to try to fi x my eye and playing inside my nose and ear. Suppose something went wrong, what would happen to me then? Hey, wait a minute. I hope all you Pentecostal and people of faith out there do not think I lack faith.

If you knew me, you would agree that I cannot afford any trial-and-error when it comes to my health. That is why I picked the best doctor in town, whose operations and procedures are sure and have medications with no side effects. His name is Dr. Jesus Christ. Even though I trust him to use natural science to take care of my health at times, this time, knowing how I got sick, I decided to let him end the job he began and not use any other doctor.

This is not to say I don't go to hospital for anything serious. Do not sit and die thinking you are applying faith when your faith is not strong enough to get you through. When you need a doctor, I pray you will have discernment to go see a doctor, because it is God who gave natural science its place to take care of us. I hope you get this clear and seek proper medical attention when necessary. But for me, I thought to myself, why do I need a physical remedy to a spiritual problem, and not seek God for my answer? It was good that I visited the doctor. At least he told me how bad my condition was so I could know how to direct my prayers. I went to the church and after three days of prayer,

I was okay again, thanks to Dr. Jesus. My eye problem, though physical, did not arise because of a physical incident so it was wise for me to counter the pain through the power of prayers. I am glad that today I can share God's miracle with you because I chose to put my faith in him in my time of need.

There are many dreadful things the devil has done to me and others that I know of, and there are many other stories I have heard about how wicked the devil is in ravaging the lives of good and innocent people – including Christians and pastors!

The truth is that the devil does not care whether you are innocent, poor, widow, orphan, housewife, president, student or choir member. The attacks of the devil come to everyone in spite of status, color, race, religion and position. Is there any hope for people since even Christians and pastors can be attacked and become victims? There are lots of Christians and pastors out there who are not living for God. Many people who claim to be Christians do not even go to church regularly. They are just Christians by membership or by name – they are not true believers.

The devil can attack Christians and pastors every day, but

true Christians and pastors can overcome the attacks of the devil. As a matter of fact, there are those the devil would be very careful around because if he dared to attack them, he's the one who will suffer. If you are a Christian or pastor, you need to be one of those the devil fears.

The Bible says we should put on the whole armor of God and stand against the wiles of the devil. We are reminded that our fight is not against flesh and blood, but against powers and principalities, against spiritual wickedness in high places. Because of the seriousness and enormity of the battle, Christians are ordered to muster themselves and prepare for war.

Whether they like it or not, the battle began upon their profession of faith in the Lord. And if we must survive the attacks or win the battle, we need special fortification that only comes from the Lord and Captain in battle – even the Lord Jesus Christ.

The Bible also says that we should resist the devil and it will flee from us. I tell you. God has given us power to overcome the devil if we are in Jesus. The Scriptures say we can do great deeds to gain wealth for ourselves and to render casualties to the devil's camp if we abide in the Lord. We are like warriors, but a kind of war in which we are more than conquerors in Christ Jesus, because he won the battle more than 2000 years ago.

Let me make this clear to you, just because Christians have God on their side, it does not mean that they sit back and not get prepared for battle. Being on any battle field and not geared up properly and ready to fight can only be seen as a suicide.

All Christians must be ready to guard what God has given them by fighting the devil to keep it. They must also design strategies to strike the devil first before he can attack them and cause any harm. Christians are warriors, as a matter fact, everyone on earth is preserved because of the presence and prayers of Christians.

Being a Christian, and especially a pastor, is not easy. The truth is, all Christians are targets of attack. Pastors are very vulnerable to attacks because they are prime targets for the devil. They are a threat to the devil and his kingdom. Pastors lead people to the saving knowledge of Jesus Christ and the devil hates that.

Pastors can reverse the curse of the devil. They can save people who are dying, through prayers and other ministry. Communities are transformed, and taboos that kept people in bondage for years are broken, and the sick are healed. God can use pastors as his special agents to usher in the kingdom of God and bring positive change. No wonder the devil strategically attacks the pastors. The devil knows that when one pastor's life and ministry is destroyed, he has succeeded greatly because now he can keep the followers under bondage.

The devil will use sex, pride, money, power and personal weaknesses to get pastors down. While it is true that we have growing churches all around the world, it is also sadly true that the devil has overcome many pastors, destroyed their ministries and even killed some. Some pastors seemed to be useless now; they are better off dead than alive.

Irrespective of all the devil can do, I encourage you to find God, hold onto him and you will succeed. If you are a believer, please hold onto your righteousness because it is a weapon against the devil. Sin will only open a door for the advance of the devil. It is better to keep the devil out of your life than to let him spoil many things before you start to fight back. If you are caught up in such a situation, hope is here for you – do not give up or give in. You must get yourself together. The fight is on.

If you have not known God personally for yourself, God is ready to accept you. You can give your life to him now. Just talk to him and say you are sorry for all your wrongdoings, ask for forgiveness and repent. If you do not mind, why don't you pause for a moment and begin to ask God to come into your life. You can do that now. God is waiting for you.

If you do that, God will be your God today and you can start a new life in him. With God now, you and rest of the believers around the world can fight the devil until he flees from your life. God is your help. Are you the type who has known God for some time but conditions are shaking your faith in Him and maybe right now you are not that sure whether there is God? Like I said above, you too can find God today and he will forgive you of your disbelief and help you. Be strong in the Lord.

Whether you are a strong believer, a new believer, pastor, church leader or some old Christian, know that the attacks of the devil are real and that you must take your stand against the advance of the enemy before it is too late. I urge you also to pray for yourself, pray for others, pray for God to help them in their times of need. I want to also ask you to pray for unbelievers, all those who have not surrendered their lives to God as their personal savior and Lord. Know that you can be an intercessor – others can depend on you. As you pray for someone, God will have another person pray for you as well. I implore you today to take your stand against the devil and do not let him destroy you. If you believe that, say amen – Amen!

# CHAPTER TWENTY

## You are Not Alone

I do not know what you are going through as you read this book; but I want you to know that you are not alone. As a matter of fact, there are many others around the world going through similar situations. There are those who have given up the fight and let things be – they say "whatever happens happen". They have lost all hope and just sit back and wait for the worst.

Even though some people are not very strong and feel they cannot take it anymore, they have not given up hope. They are still in the fight. They press forward in spite of the losses they have experienced. They take time to remember the gains they have enjoyed and all they do now is fight on until help can come.

There are others still who dare not let the devil or any situation steal their joy, family or possession. They actively fight for what is rightfully theirs in the Lord. They pray daily and live a life of righteousness, even though they are not perfect. They fight a good fight. They work out their salvation and enjoy times of fellowship with the Lord and others. These sorts of people are too dangerous to handle. Any attacks on them means heavy counter attacks to the devil. They are a ready army for the Lord.

## WHERE IS GOD?

Let it be made clear to you that you are not alone in your struggle in life. Others are going through the same problem. I want you to know that God makes others around the world who you do not even know to pray for you every day. So please hang in there.

Life is like school. There is a curriculum, teachers who teach it and students who should take tests to determine how much of the lesson they retain. Those who pass the test are promoted to the next level and get closer to graduation. But those who fail the tests are retained until they can pass. Those students may decide to study to pass or drop out of school, and complain about how hard it is.

Now let me ask you something: if you see life as a school, what student are you? The curriculum and test are the same. Are you making good grades, complaining, fussing, or dropping out? Okay, let me put it this way to help you better understand. God is the school president. The world is the school; our place in life is the classroom. The tests are the different issues we face daily in life – the good, the bad, the ugly, and the shameful. All these various things and the people we experience are the tests. Our grades are our attitude and response to the situations. The devil at times and the angels administer the tests to us. The curriculum is as lengthy as our lifetime.

Now that I have clarified this, you can go on and answer my question. If life is a school, what student are you? I hope you are not the student who cheats on the test like people who consult spirits, witch doctors, diviners, soothsayers and mediums or read daily horoscopes to know what life brings and what is in their stars.

Knowledge of your life and future alone will not suffice to protect you or give you better life. That is why you and I have to try to find God. Instead of the creation of God to find answers that only God alone can properly answer; we go through life without God. The Bible says that [32] when you go through the fi re, I am there, never will I leave you or forsake you." I am glad that we have this assurance. We are not alone my dear friends.

In the midst of all the different troubles you and I face in life, I want to tell you that you are not alone. There are other brothers and sisters who are in similar situations. There are people who care about you. Many people are praying for you – even some of the people you do not know. People like me and many others intercede daily as the Lord directs us in prayers. You are not alone. God has not forgotten you. Please don't let your problems make you forget about God.

I understand that there are times when God seems too far away. At other times it feels that no one cares; please do not believe the lie of the devil. I have had my share of troubles in life. Some people played to my weaknesses and magnified my flaws in my life and ministry as if they were perfect. There are some people who are just so busy finding faults to belittle others and tear them down, as if there is nothing else meaningful in the world to do. Instead of giving their time and energy to volunteer for a worthy cause or invest in something, they seek the downfall of other people. What a tragedy!

Some people in my church rose up against me and told church members that God had left me, and that God has given them my vision while I was on a mission trip. They stopped communicating with me and did things I would not approve. They practically tarnished my reputation before the church and sidelined my family in the church. They said lot of evil things about me that sounded so real to the extent that some trusted people began to doubt my integrity. As a matter of fact, these haters made a lot of church members turn against me.

But after a time of fasting, prayer and hard work, the Lord turned everything around. I don't know what you are going through; but I felt my world was falling apart. I was in the midst of people, yet I was lonely. While in the middle of all this, I too remembered that I was not alone – and that helped me to focus. Just like I am telling you, I assured myself and knew help was on the way.

Help is on the way for you too. Hang in there! Whatever life brings you, remember that you are not alone. You have people. You have God, and of course, you have me as your wingman. I believe with God you and I can make it in Jesus name.

Rise up and shine! You can make it again. You can come to yourself again. Put yourself together. Come on, rise up! If you have lost ABC and even D, it's okay. Sorry, life is full of problems and disappointments, but there is success as well.

If you experienced bad times, it does not in any way mean that good times will not come again. Don't let anyone, especially the devil and his cohorts, lie to you. You are too big, too good, too smart and too charming for these little cheap lies. You are better than that. The fact that you are not dead yet and still have your good senses enough to read this book tells me that your salvation is on the way. The plan to rescue you is underway. God has already dispatched a special team to come to your aid. I know that you can make it. You are not alone! You are not alone!

# CHAPTER TWENTY-ONE

## Press Forward

The best person in Christianity to whom the phrase "press forward" can be attributed was a man with a unique story. Saul of Tarsus, as he was previously called, was a religious, ambitious intellectual Pharisee – one of the highest Jewish religious orders during his time – and a charismatic character. Saul wanted to make sure that no one, be it a Christian or any gossiper, and carry news around about Jesus' resurrection or his teachings.

Saul got orders from the religious rulers to flog, arrest, and imprison anyone talking about Jesus, his message or resurrection. With such power, he chased Christ's followers all over Israel. When people were in church and they heard that Saul was coming, everyone including the pastor would run for their lives. He was so wicked to the early Christians.

But on one of his expeditions to Damascus, Saul met Jesus Christ and his life was forever changed. From the blinding experience he had, the wicked Saul of Tarsus was converted to Christianity and given a new name – Paul, the Apostle Paul. Paul was the disciple of Jesus who took the good news of the gospel out of Jerusalem to Macedonia, Antioch, Thessalonica, Philippi,

Corinth, Galatia, Ephesus, and finally to Rome. He was the one who encouraged the disciples, even though persecution was forcing them to run, to preach to others outside of Jerusalem. He became the pioneer of the churches in the Greco-Roman world. No wonder he is call the "Apostle to the Gentiles," a title he rightfully deserved.

Paul experienced some problems with the other disciples because they were afraid of him at first and they did not trust him. Paul got in trouble with governments and was jailed many times because he preached the gospel of Jesus Christ. God used Paul to raise the dead, and miracles accompanied his ministry. Towns and cities were upside down because Apostle Paul was in town; people felt the power of God everywhere he went. He was a "celebrity" in his own right even though he chose to be very humble.

Paul deliberated with religious leaders and convinced many that Jesus Christ was the real way and not the law, especially knowing how they had magnified the law inappropriately. He lectured intellectuals in synagogues and temples; he challenged gods. Professors and intellectuals who never wanted to convert had to either dismiss him or run away before he turned them into believers. He was shipwrecked. He was bitten by a deadly venomous snake. He was jailed and locked in shackles with many guards around him, but God delivered him from them all.

Paul would boast of nothing except the cross and the glory. He ascended into the third heavens. He was a powerful minister. He raised and nurtured young leaders like Timothy,

Titus and Philemon. He raised female pastors, unlike others who felt women should not do anything in the church. Paul lived on his own handy work and did not live on church offerings and tithes.

It was this same Paul who made this powerful statement when he said, [33] forgetting those things which are behind and reaching forward to those things which are ahead." What an awesome thing to say! Paul enjoyed his portion of leading a wrong life that he believed in so much until he had a rude awakening. I pray that God will give some of us rude awakenings to help us catch the vision and live it. If you do not know God I pray that you will receive in a gentle way; if not, may God give you some rude awaken that will rock your world forever.

He enjoyed the call of God and he led many to God. Paul did church planting, leadership training, raised special love offerings, and was harassed over and over again because of the gospel. He chased out demons –Paul was on top of things! But Paul, regardless of his past, looked intently for a future that was far better than his past and present. It was for that future, that purpose, that goal, the prize that the great apostle said, [34] forgetting those things which are behind and reaching forward to those things which are ahead." Today Christians and many leaders around the world choose to learn from Paul for leadership and service. Because Paul believed in his vision so much such that he was willing to die for what he believed. He lived for his vision so much that during one of his missions to Rome, even his mentor, Barnabas, left him because of the risk involved. Paul was daring!

With all these accolades and standing ovations, we can give the Apostle Paul, they really do not seem to matter to him more than pursuing what is ahead and not focusing on the past, nor the present. When he talked about some of his experiences, it was only for the sole purpose of informing his audience that God was glorified in his sufferings.

Raising up men and women in the ministry, he fought hard to be that example he wanted them to be. At one time he told young Timothy "follow me as I follow Christ." When we are moving forward, others will follow. Everyone wants to follow a leader who is moving ahead.

Our speed and bright star may be something others might be envious of. Because they do not know how to handle our bright star, some of them begin to fight against us. Do not worry, they will soon get used to it. All you have to do is say to yourself is, "I am "pressing forward, backwards never," and live your life. Remember, it is about you; not them.

The Apostle Paul forgot about all that had happened over the years that he had the right to brag about. Instead, he told everyone to "press forward." Paul properly understood that what was behind was in the past. He knew that yesterday's tomorrow is today, and that today would be tomorrow's yesterday.

That is why we should all "press forward" because we should not dwell on the many things behind us. Some things that are in the past should never resurface again – never! Behind us could be a time of merit, joy, accomplishments and a lot of good time. But the past might hold a lot of grief, sorrow, frustration, bad relationships, great loss, and some really shameful things we do not want anyone to bring up. On account of this, we all should forget the past and look forward to a bright future.

The hope of a better tomorrow can help us go through any difficult problem. All things around us could be very negative, but when we have just a little hope, it can reenergize us to steer forward amidst dangerous storms and rough seas. If the truth be told, there are some conditions that are so bad that it is hard to believe that we can find our way out, but with a little hope and faith, God can help us see light, be it dim, at the end of the tunnel.

When we have made up our minds to press forward, we can receive a special synergy to do the impossible. We can look straight in the face of things that want to destroy us and say with boldness, "I am not afraid of you!" We will fight. If things are so bad that we can fight no more, we will resolve just to hang in there until help arrives. Today I want to challenge you, do not give up. Press forward. I understand life is difficult. Life is not fair. People cannot always be trusted. We have personal failures I know that. But despite all of the reasons we have as grounds to fail, I encourage you to press forward. Press forward. Help is on the way.

As I write this book, I too have issues. I am caught up in a lot of things that only God can get me through, but I have decided I will not give up. I have plenty of weaknesses as a person. I will not pretend to anyone that I have mastered the art of leadership and piety and present myself in a way that is not honest. I keep it real.

Yet in the midst of all this, I pressed forward to complete this project. I have failures as a man, plenty of failures as a husband and father. I have to balance church, mission and family. I also need time for myself. There is a special call of God upon my life that pushes me and connects to everything else.

Therefore, I take courage in the Lord and enjoy consolation from friends and family. Yes, life is not easy. We all know that. So why do you cry like there is no hope? Why do you act like you are the only one suffering? Have you ever thought about the suffering masses in Africa, a rich continent yet extreme poverty reigns? Have you considered India, China and Latin America, to see all the vices of society that makes life difficult for people? Even in the great Untied States of America, there are still the homeless people and hungry children, even though America uses more than half of the world's resources!

What more can I tell you to help you understand? You may feel like you have the right to express your dislikes about the world, your president, political leaders, and even local leaders in both public and private sectors; I agree with you. But regardless of all that, I sternly say to you, do not give up, do not give in. No matter how long or how hard it is, press forward and God will make a way for you. As He opened up the Red Sea for Israel to cross through and delivered them from the hands of Egypt, God can still open doors for you. As He stopped the sun for Joshua to defeat the enemy, he can redeem the days for you. As he turned Esther, a teenage refugee girl, into a daring queen, he can turn your situation around. He gave Naomi beauty for ashes through

Ruth and Boaz. He gave Joseph a butler. Come on, God will make a way. If he did it for the others, why not you and me? Let us hold on to him.

Believe, follow his lead and you will be surprised at how wonderful the Lord can make things work out for good for you. He can make the mess into a message. He can make the test into testimony. I say to you, believe God. When you ask, "Where is God?" please understand that God is there. Whether life is good or bad, God is! Believe it. Receive it! God bless you.

# Bibliography

1 www.seti.org

2 Anonymous Liberian wise saying

3 Psalm 46:1, Holy Bible, New International Version, Published by Zondervan 1984, Grand Rapids, Michigan

4 Justice: Merriam-Webster's Collegiate Dictionary Tenth Edition, Merriam-webster, Incorporated, Springfield, Massachusetts, U.S.A

5 Justice: Merriam-Webster's Collegiate Dictionary Tenth Edition, Merriam-webster, Incorporated, Springfield, Massachusetts, U.S.A

6 Job 24:12-14 Holy Bible, New International Version, Published by Zondervan 1984, Grand Rapids, Michigan

7 Matthew 18: 23-31 Holy Bible, New International Version, Published by Zondervan 1984, Grand Rapids, Michigan

8 Liberia National Anthem- http://www.lyricsondemand.com/miscellaneouslyrics/nationalanthemslyrics/liberianationalanthemlyrics.html Composed in 1860 by Daniel Bashiel Warner (1813 - 1880) Third President of Liberia 1864 - 1868 Music by Olmstead Luca (b. 1836)

9 Matthew 7:12 - Holy Bible, New International Version, Published by Zondervan 1984, Grand Rapids, Michigan

10 Job 29: 4, 7, 12 - Holy Bible, New International Version, Published by Zondervan 1984, Grand Rapids, Michigan

11 Ecclesiastes 3:12 - Holy Bible, New International Version, Published by Zondervan 1984, Grand Rapids, Michigan

12 Genesis 2: 7-9, 15-18, 22; 3:8-12 - Holy Bible, New International Version, Published by Zondervan 1984, Grand Rapids, Michigan

13 Genesis 3:8-12 - Holy Bible, New International Version, Published by Zondervan 1984, Grand Rapids, Michigan

14 1 Samuel 2: 12-34, 4 - Holy Bible, New International Version, Published by Zondervan 1984, Grand Rapids, Michigan

15 Proverbs 13:24 Holy Bible, New International Version, Published by Zondervan 1984, Grand Rapids, Michigan

16 Joshua 9:14 Holy Bible, New International Version, Published by Zondervan 1984, Grand Rapids, Michigan

17 2 Samuel 11 & 12 – David and Bathsheba - Holy Bible, New International Version, Published by Zondervan 1984, Grand Rapids, Michigan

18 Philippians 2 :1-11 Holy Bible, New International Version, Published by Zondervan 1984, Grand Rapids, Michigan

19 Isaiah 59:1-2 Holy Bible, New International Version, Published by Zondervan 1984, Grand Rapids, Michigan

20 I John 1:8 Holy Bible, New International Version, Published by Zondervan 1984, Grand Rapids, Michigan

21 http://wwrn.org/articles/33785/ Kenya: Bishop Shot Dead in Night Raid at Church Fred Mukinda ("Daily Nation," July 4, 2010)

22 Luke 17:11-19 Holy Bible, New International Version, Published by Zondervan 1984, Grand Rapids, Michigan

## WHERE IS GOD?

23 James 1:17 Holy Bible, New International Version, Published by Zondervan 1984, Grand Rapids, Michigan

24 Romans 8: 32 Holy Bible, New International Version, Published by Zondervan 1984, Grand Rapids, Michigan

25 James 1: 2 – 4 Holy Bible, New International Version, Published by Zondervan 1984, Grand Rapids, Michigan

26 Job 1: 1 – 12 Holy Bible, New International Version, Published by Zondervan 1984, Grand Rapids, Michigan

27 Job 2: 1-10 Holy Bible, New International Version, Published by Zondervan 1984, Grand Rapids, Michigan

28 Romans 3:23 Holy Bible, New International Version, Published by Zondervan 1984, Grand Rapids, Michigan

29 Romans 6:23 Holy Bible, New International Version, Published by Zondervan 1984, Grand Rapids, Michigan

30 Anonymous Liberian proverb

31 Philippians 3:13 Holy Bible, New International Version, Published by Zondervan 1984, Grand Rapids, Michigan

32 Hebrews13:5 Holy Bible, New International Version, Published by Zondervan 1984, Grand Rapids, Michigan
"If you're not inside, you don't know". – Anonymous Liberian proverb

33 Philippians 3:12 Holy Bible, New International Version, Published by Zondervan 1984, Grand Rapids, Michigan

34 Philippians 3:12 Holy Bible, New International Version, Published by Zondervan 1984, Grand Rapids, Michigan

# Born To Take Charge

I encourage you to check out my second book **"BORN TO TAKE CHARGE"**. It is a piece on self-discovery, leadership and taking charge to live a fulfilled life. The book is divided into six parts.

**Part 1** says that God is not done with me yet. It is good to recognize our situation and admit our humanity; when we do, we take a good step in the right direction.

**Part 2** talks about sleeping at the wrong time. While others are making great strides and getting ahead in life, sleeping at the wrong time can make us leave behind. It can even make us to experience trouble. Instead of sleeping, we must apply our mind.

**Part 3** teaches us to drop the stuff we carry around. This includes our bad thoughts, bad friends and even the bad places we go.

**Part 4** reminds us that we were born to take charge. We are called to bear fruit, multiply, fill the earth, subdue it and have dominion. We are supposed to be the head, why are some of us behind? Let's take charge.

**Part 5** says even though we were born to take charge but we must work hard and pray hard in order to be successful in life. Life demands hard work; no food for lazy man.

**Part 6** acknowledges the need for God in order to live a fulfilled life. It teaches us to personally ask God to fix us up in our limitations. We all have things that put us down, God can fix us up to become new people.

I believe **"BORN TO TAKE CHARGE"** will be a great book to help you take charge of your life, pursue your purpose, and reach your destiny. I will be waiting to hear your story. God bless you.

# WHERE IS GOD?

# ABOUT THE AUTHOR

Rev. James C. Nyemah is the first grandchild of Ma Phebe of Gbiso, a great woman of God known for prayers and miracles in Maryland County, Liberia. He is the founder and Senior Pastor of Africa Faith Expressions, a church that touches the African community in Arizona. He is the first Liberian pastor to open a church in Phoenix, Arizona. Here, some call him Brother James or Pastor James; either way, it is the same guy. He is a community man.

During the rape case of an 8-year old Liberian girl who was molested by three boys in 2009, a story that made national and international headlines, Pastor James stood up and advocated for the family of the victim and his community.

From 2005 – 2009, his church was greatly involved in the integration process of the West African refugees. He worked with humanitarian agencies in the Valley like the International Rescue Committee and Catholic Charities to help his people.

In 2005, Bro. James received his first degree, a BA in Biblical and Christian Studies with emphasis in Inter-Cultural Ministry, from Grand Canyon University. He has a distinct calling from God directing his life.

In Arizona, he uses sports in evangelism to touch lives. He loves young people. Thanks to Rev. Nyemah, today the African community uses Cactus Park on the weekends for sports and pass-time.

In 2008, he made his first missionary journey to Liberia, West Africa, and started three churches in rural Liberia. He has a heart for missions. Since 2011, he has conducted several leadership conferences for pastors and community leaders all over Liberia, touching 500 to 1000 pastors at a time, teaching God's word and biblical leadership. You can be a part of this today.

Rev. James's organization, Missions Liberia (ml), is known for leadership training and community development. He believes good leadership and community empowerment is the best way for Liberia to move forward. He is working on other projects for education, micro-finance, sports, youth empowerment, and childcare programs to help rebuild Liberia.

Rev. James Nyemah and his wife, Lucy, live in Glendale, Arizona. Their daughter, Precious, is a freshman at the University of Arizona in Tucson. Watch out for his next book: "Born to Take Charge" a piece on purpose and leadership to live a fulfilled life.

Other Titles

**BORN TO TAKE CHARGE**

COMING SOON!!!!!

**ESTABLISH ME**

www.ingramcontent.com/pod-product-compliance
Lightning Source LLC
Chambersburg PA
CBHW060538100426
42743CB00009B/1567